JUDGMENT BUT HOPE

Isaiah Part 1

ISAIAH—"The Holy One of Israel"

You're about to study the crown jewel of Old Testament prophets, a book that will fill you with awe as you come face to face with "the Holy One of Israel"—a phrase Isaiah repeats 25 times but which is found only 6 more times in the Bible and only in the Old Testament: once in Kings, three times in the Psalms, and twice in Jeremiah.

God's holiness is a recurring theme. Between 739 B.C. and 681 B.C., Isaiah watched the spiritual and moral deterioration of the Southern Kingdom of Judah and preached the "vision" he received during the reigns of Uzziah Jotham, Ahaz, and Hezekiah (Isaiah 1:1) and likely continued to preach it for part of Manasseh's rule (697-642 B.C.)—possibly the most wicked king of Judah. He knew that no matter how bad things got, Jehovah would ultimately humiliate sin and exalt justice and righteousness. He warns God's people of approaching captivity and the surrounding nations of approaching judgments. But beyond judgment he always looked to the hope of the coming Messiah, His universal kingdom (from sea to sea), justice and restoration!

Jesus quotes Isaiah extensively and Isaiah's name is mentioned 22 times in the New Testament, all associated with prophecies of the Messiah's comings. This program (Part 1) will carry us through the first section of the book (39 chapters). Just as the Bible divides into 39 books of the Old Testament and 27 of the New, Isaiah divides into two sections of 39 chapters and 27 chapters.

There couldn't be a more relevant time to study Isaiah. We're living in identical times—apostasy from the true faith and consequent idolatry of one sort or another, disrespect for justice and the sanctity of human life and marriage, and nations rising up against nations.

We don't know how all this is going to shake out for our nation or any other, but we do know we're reliving Isaiah's times and God wants us to relive his ministry. Like Isaiah, we can trust that the Holy One of Israel will continue to judge sin and promote His love and justice. And we can look to the Messiah's second coming. It's an awesome and exciting time to live in Beloved, a time for us to speak the prophetic Word of God to everyone we know! The message is the same—approaching judgment or salvation.

You'll see this every day as you join with us to learn the book of Isaiah. May the Lord richly bless you in this inductive study!

Kay

INSIDE

PRECEPTS FOR LIFE™
Study Companion

This Bible study material was designed for use with the TV and Radio teaching program, Precepts for Life™ with renowned Bible study teacher Kay Arthur, a production of Precept Ministries International. This inductive 30-minute daily Bible study program airs on many satellite, cable, and broadcast stations, and on the internet at **www.preceptsforlife.com.**

As with all Inductive Bible studies, the best way to use the material is to complete the assignments in each lesson before listening or watching the PFL program for that day. These programs are also available on DVD and CD at **www.preceptsforlife.com** or by phone (1.800.763.1990 for television viewers or 1.800.734.7707 for radio listeners). For more information about the Precept Inductive Bible Study Method and Precept Ministries International, visit **www.preceptsforlife.com.**

These materials are also useful for Bible study apart from the Precepts for Life™ programs. We hope you'll find them valuable for studying God's Word and that your walk will be strengthened by the life-changing Truth you'll encounter each day.

Isaiah Part 1—Judgment – But Hope STUDY COMPANION
Published by Precept Ministries of Reach Out, Inc.
P. O. Box 182218
Chattanooga, TN 37422

ISBN–13: 978-1-934884-40-9

All Scripture quotations, unless otherwise indicated, are taken from the *NEW AMERICAN STANDARD BIBLE*®(NASB) © Copyright1960, 1962, 1963, 1968, 1971, 1972, 1973, 1975, 1977, 1995 by the. Used by permission. (www.lockman.org)

Copyright © 2008 Precept Ministries International

Printed in the United States of America

Precept, Precept Ministries International, Precept Ministries International the Inductive Bible Study People, the Plumb Bob design, Precept Upon Precept, In & Out, Sweeter than Chocolate!, Cookies on the Lower Shelf, Precepts For Life, Precepts From God's Word and Transform Student Ministries are trademarks of Precept Ministries International.

Listen! The Lord Has Spoken!

SYNOPSIS

Did you know that Jesus and His apostles quoted more from Isaiah than from any other prophet? What did this man who lived more than 700 years before Christ say that was applicable to generations so far ahead of his time, even to us today?

More than ever, we need to know the truth—God's truth. Our study in Isaiah will provide deep insight into the unchanging character of God and His plan for His people. You will learn about His holiness, His righteous judgments, and His provision of a Redeemer through Jesus Christ. You will see that He is the Lord and there is no other (Isaiah 45:6).

TODAY'S TEXT
Isaiah 1:1-4

 Where's That Verse?

CROSS-REFERENCES

Isaiah 45:5

Exodus 4:22

Deuteronomy 28:1-2, 15, 20

Psalms 46:10; 119:104

John 1:11-12

QUESTIONS

1. Read Isaiah 1:1-4, asking the 5 W and H questions (who, what, when, where, why, and how) to determine the context. What do you learn about Isaiah and when he delivers his message? Who does his vision concern?

2. Who is speaking in verse 2? What is He talking about?

3. What do you learn about Israel from these verses? List everything this nation has done to God.

4. Now consider Israel's relationship to God as "son" (Exodus 4:22) and how this relates to you. According to John 1:11-12, who are God's children?

5. Read Exodus 4:22. Why did God release His "son" from slavery? How does the Israel Isaiah describes contrast with this physically freed son?

6. Spend the remainder of your study time today evaluating your life. Used for both people and animals, "know" in Isaiah 1:3 includes the idea of recognition. Are you a child of God? Do you recognize God—His character, ways, and commands?

7. Have you, like Israel, rebelled and turned away from God? Are you weighed down with judgments on your bad choices?

8. Jesus said that whatever you ask in His name He will do for the glory of God. Ask Him for diligence, perseverance, and strength to commit to this study. Pray that the Spirit of truth will open the eyes of your heart to receive His Word and grant you the power to live it out.

Prayer

Lord you spoke and speak through your eternal Word. Although Isaiah delivered Your message thousands of years ago, You have not changed; You have the same plan for Your people to be holy. I want to live the life that pleases You. Help me diligently spend time meditating on these truths in Isaiah and be transformed by them. In Jesus' name, Amen.

PROGRAM 2

TODAY'S TEXT

Isaiah 1:1-6

Where's That Verse?

CROSS-REFERENCES

Isaiah 45:5

Genesis 15:9-21

Exodus 4:22-23; 6:2-7

Psalm 38:3-9

Romans 1:16; 9:3-5

Philippians 2:10-11, 3:4-6

Did You Know?

Jews consider "LORD" (YHWH: Yahweh, Jehovah) to be the most sacred name for God, so sacred they won't even speak it (they substitute Adonai). When you see "Lord" in your Bible spelled with a capital "L" and the rest small letters, it represents the Hebrew "Adonai." When it's in all capital letters, it represents "Yahweh."

Sin's Painful Consequences

SYNOPSIS

Are you living with regrets, painful consequences from rash, unwise **decisions?** Have you willfully rebelled against God's absolute and authoritative truth? Although the Lord judged Israel terribly when they abandoned Him, He always held out hope to them—a hope we can share: God keeps His promise to save.

QUESTIONS

1. Read Isaiah 1:1-6. Once again note who is speaking, to whom, and when. What has Israel done?

2. How is God described in these verses? (Read the **Did You Know?** box for additional insight.)

3. What do you learn about Israel's sin from the question posed in verse 5? Who has "stricken" Israel for their rebellion?

4. What are the ramifications of their sin?

5. Look up Psalm 38:3—King David's account following his adulterous affair with Bathsheba. How did he suffer for his sin?

6. Why does God discipline His children for sin?

7. In Exodus 6:2-7 God is speaking to Moses about the liberation of Israel from Egypt. Read these verses and answer the following questions:
   a. What did Israel suffer?
   b. What did God promise their forefathers?
   c. What is His plan for redemption? (Note what He promises to do.)
   d. What does all this teach you about God?

8. Now read Romans 1:16 and 9:3-5. What special privileges did God grant Israel?

9. If God remembers His covenant and wants to redeem His people, what can you conclude with respect to yourself? Can anything prevent Him from fulfilling His promises?

Prayer
Lord, I confess that I have done things my way—in my own strength and understanding. I empathize with David's pain and know I can't cure myself. But I also know that You are Jehovah-Rapha—the God who heals. I humbly submit my life and choices to You. By faith, I ask for Your redeeming power in my life for Your glory. In Jesus' name, Amen.

"Come now, and let us reason together"

SYNOPSIS

What's going on in your culture today and are you part of it? Do you "play church" thinking your prayers are just hitting the ceiling? At least 72 times God declares His will in Isaiah and almost 60 times He tells His people to listen. If you hear, He can make your sins "white as snow."

Where's That Verse?

CROSS-REFERENCES

Genesis 18:20; 19:4

Psalms 51:4, 7, 12; 139:7-12

Romans 8:17

Galatians 4:7

Hebrews 13:4

1 John 1:9

QUESTIONS

1. Today let's analyze Isaiah 1:2-3, 7-28, focusing particularly on what the Lord says to Israel. Look for imperatives (instructions/commands) and propositions (declarative sentences) that give you insight into God's character.

2. How is Israel's land described in this chapter? What is happening? (Note: "daughter of Zion" and "faithful city" are synonyms for Jerusalem.)

3. How is Israel's spiritual condition further described in these verses? What do "Sodom" and "Gomorrah" imply?"

4. What does God say about their worship?

5. What do you learn about Israel's political leaders? How does it compare with your nation's leaders?

6. What must Israel do to be cleansed of their sin (1:18-19, 27)?

7. What will happen if they do not obey the Lord (1:20, 28)?

8. What do you learn about God from these verses? Why does He leave survivors in Israel? How does He deal with sin and with repentance?

9. Read Psalm 51. What does David acknowledge about his sin? Although he committed adultery, deceived, and murdered, who does he say he sinned against? What does he ask God to do? What does God delight in?

10. Read 1 John 1:9—a promise to believers. The Greek verb translated "confess" (homologeo) means "to say the same thing." What does God do for those who confess their sins?

11. What is God saying to you today? Do you need to repent of anything? What steps do you need to take to be right with Him?

Did You Know?

The Hebrew translated by "Lord of hosts" is Yahweh [Jehovah] Sabaoth, meaning the ruler of hosts—armies of angels. God is supreme commander.

Prayer

Lord, You are holy and cannot tolerate sin; yet You provided for my sin through Your Son Jesus Christ so I can walk in righteousness. I confess that I have been worldly and hypocritical. Forgive my sins and cleanse me from their stains. Create in me Your passion for purity and renew my strength to walk in the power of the Holy Spirit. In Jesus' matchless name I pray, Amen.

Where's That Verse?

CROSS-REFERENCES

Isaiah 1:2, 4, 18, 21

2 Kings 19:22

Psalm 25:4; 71:22; 78:41; 89:18; 119:105; 135:18

Jeremiah 50:29; 51:5

Daniel 11:32

Mark 9:44

Luke 13:3

John 8:32, 44

Romans 15:3

1 Corinthians 10:11

Ephesians 5:26

Hebrews 1:2

1 Peter 1:23; 5:8

Revelation 20:10

Did You Know?

The "Holy One of Israel" is used 25 times in the book of Isaiah, yet only six other times in the Word of God (see 2 Kings 19:22; Psalm 71:22, 78:41, and 89:18; and Jeremiah 50:29 and 51:5).

Timeline

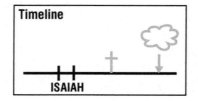

ISAIAH

In the last days...

SYNOPSIS

Why do terrorist attacks, earthquakes, hurricanes, tsunamis, and other large-scale shocks incite fear and panic? Underneath the crippling sense of powerlessness against death closing in, is it the terrible realization that a holy God is judging justly? When the day of the Lord comes, will you be gripped with terror or rejoicing?

QUESTIONS

1. Read Isaiah 1:24-31 and 2:1-5. As you observe the text, mark the following key words:

    a. *Repentant* and (synonym) *return* with a red U-turn symbol

    b. Time phrases with a green clock (e.g. *then, when, last days,* etc.)

    c. *Jerusalem* (city of righteousness, faithful city, mountain, Zion) with a blue Star of David

    d. *Nations* with a brown underline, shaded green

    Marking repeated key words and phrases helps unlock the meaning of a text. It slows you down so you can focus on the text then afterward it enables you to quickly compile a list of facts or terms from a chapter. Always ask the 5W and H questions while marking to understand what you're marking.

    Because you will mark some words throughout your study, consider creating a bookmark with a list of these "keys" and their respective markings.

2. What is God going to do to His "adversaries" according to 1:24-25? Based on prior verses, who does this group include?

3. During this judgment, what will happen in Jerusalem to the:

    a. repentant?

    b. sinners?

4. What will burn and for how long? What does this tell you about the things the world values?

5. Look up Luke 13:3. According to Jesus what happens to those who don't repent of their sins?

6. What will occur in the last days according to chapter 2? What did you learn from marking nations?

7. Record a theme for chapter 1 on your **At A Glance** chart.

8. Have you heard the Word of the Lord today? Will you be among the redeemed? Have you warned others that judgment is coming?

Prayer

Lord my ardent prayer is for You to teach me Your ways through Your Word. I want to be found faithful and stand approved before You on the day of judgment. It's a sobering message to know that many will burn forever, apart from Your presence. Help me sound forth the very Word You have given me. In Jesus' mighty name, Amen.

The Day of Reckoning

SYNOPSIS

How can you possibly have peace in such a cruel, unjust world? Brutal stories, crimes against children, war atrocities and more dominate newspapers and networks around the globe. You can surrender your fleshly desire to retaliate when you understand God's plan for the wicked around us. A day of reckoning is coming!

QUESTIONS

1. Read Isaiah 2:1-21 and mark **nation(s), mountain** (Jerusalem, Zion), and time phrases (*in that day, the day of reckoning*, etc.). How is the Lord described in these verses?

2. Briefly summarize the main points of the last days described in verses 1-4.

3. What does Isaiah call for in verse 5? Why is this also an appeal to Christians today?

4. Note the description of the people in verses 6-8. What do they put their trust in?

5. What happens "in that day," the "day of reckoning?"

6. Who is the Lord against? Underline every occurrence of **against** and list your observations.

7. Now read Psalm 2:1-6, Joel 3:9-21 and Revelation 11:15-18. Note events leading up to the day of the Lord and what happens when God's mountain is established. Mark references to the nations for a better understanding of God's dealings with them.

8. How should you respond to the truths about the day of the Lord?

9. Are you full of pride? Do you trust your intellect, abilities, resources? What happens to the proud?

10. Record a theme for chapter 2 on your **At A Glance** chart.

Prayer
Father God, I'm outraged by the horrors in the world but You are still on Your throne and will deal out justice when You want. You're faithful to Your people and do not let evil go unpunished. Keep my mind from wandering, keep me near You, and sustain me with Your Word until that terrible and glorious day. In the name of your holy Son, the Lord Jesus, Amen.

TODAY'S TEXT
Isaiah 2:1-21

Where's That Verse?
CROSS-REFERENCES

Isaiah 1:4

Psalms 2:1-6; 146:3-5

Joel 3:9-21

Amos 4:1

John 8:12

Colossians 1:13; 3:5

1 Timothy 6:10

Revelation 6:16; 11:15-18 20:11-15

Did You Know?

King Hezekiah reigned from about 730-686 B.C.; Isaiah prophesied from about 739-681 B.C. during the reigns of Uzziah, Jotham, Ahaz, and Hezekiah (kings of Judah).

PROGRAM 6

TODAY'S TEXT
Isaiah 1:2-5, 19; 2:2

Where's That Verse?

CROSS-REFERENCES
Numbers 15:30-31
Deuteronomy 7:6-11
Jeremiah 29:11
Hebrews 12:1, 5-6
1 Peter 1:1-2, 14-16; 4:17

Consent and Obey

SYNOPSIS

Why does God tell His children to "walk in a manner worthy" of the high calling on their lives (Ephesians 4:1)? Do you know what He has called you to? Many professing Christians today live ignorant of God's Word yet fully expecting to receive His blessings. When you live for Christ today, you can walk victoriously and understand the true hope of glory.

QUESTIONS

1. In Isaiah 1:2 God calls Israel "sons." Read Deuteronomy 7:6-11. Note the basis on which God chose Israel and for what purpose.
   a. What do you learn about God from this passage?
   b. What was Israel "redeemed" from?
   c. According to verse 11, what is Israel's responsibility?
   d. What does "to a thousandth generation" mean?

2. Now look up 1 Peter 1:1-2, 14-16. According to these verses, who is chosen, by whom, and for what purpose? What is their responsibility?

3. Review what you learned about Israel's condition in Isaiah 1:2-5. What had they done and how did God strike them according to verse 5?

4. What does God ask them to do in Isaiah 1:19?

5. Read Hebrews 12:1, 5-11 and again note the believer's responsibility. How does God deal with His "sons" and why?

6. What do you learn about judgment from 1 Peter 4:17? What does this reveal about God?

7. Are you living according to God's precepts for life? Is your standard God's standard – holiness?

8. "All Scripture is inspired by God and profitable for … reproof and correction…" (2 Timothy 3:16). If you're convicted of some sin, confess it to God now and tell Him you want to live as His holy child to please Him.

Prayer
Holy Father, before the foundation of the world You chose me and set me apart to be holy. Like Israel You freed me from slavery to sin. Grant me power to walk in Your ways and Your Holy Spirit to guide me to all truth. Help me respond positively to Your discipline so I'll share Your holy character and know the peaceful fruit of righteousness. In the name of Your only Son, my Lord and Savior, Amen.

Woe to the Proud

SYNOPSIS

Do political leaders truly represent the people they serve? Think about the topics that are center stage in your country. Do your leaders advocate justice and moral law, or are they merely puppets of corrupt special interest groups? Today we'll examine God's judgment on societies that abandon His Law.

QUESTIONS

1. To get into context for today's study, review Isaiah 2:12-22 to consider who the Lord humiliates.

2. What can you conclude from 2:22 about how society regarded these men?

3. Look up Psalm 146:3-7. How does this command compare with Isaiah 2:22? Who is blessed? What do you learn about the Lord?

4. Now read Isaiah 3:1-9, marking references to **_Jerusalem_** and the new key word **_woe_** with a red cloud shaded brown.

5. Who are the leaders in Jerusalem and what's going to happen to them? Who will rule in their place?

6. What did they do? List why God will judge their actions (vv. 8-9).

7. How much influence does leadership have on the moral standards of its society, good or bad?

8. Finally, look up Galatians 1:10 and Matthew 6:24. What do these verses teach about how many masters we can serve?

9. Who is leading your country and where to? What criterion determines who you support – popular opinion or God's law?

TODAY'S TEXT
Isaiah 3:1-9

 **Where's That Verse?**

CROSS-REFERENCES

Isaiah 1:1-2; 2:1-6, 12-18, 22

1 Kings 18:21

Psalms 2:4-9; 146:3-7

Matthew 6:24

Mark 16:19

Galatians 1:10

Revelation 19:11-16

Prayer
Father, I want to uncompromisingly stand for truth, integrity, and justice. Give me courage to oppose those who reject these things. Take out wicked and corrupt leaders and mercifully replace them with godly men Your people can rally behind. I pray in Jesus' name, trusting Your sovereignty over the nations, Amen.

The Lord Enters Into Judgment

 Where's That Verse?

CROSS-REFERENCES

Exodus 22:21

Hebrews 13:4

SYNOPSIS

God's chosen nation Israel—freed from slavery, led by His holy presence through the wilderness, provided His holy Law, and made victorious in their conquests – fell because their "speech and actions" were against Him (Isaiah 3:8). If God is the same yesterday, today, and forever, what does this mean for our nation? What happens when a country descends into immorality and decadence?

QUESTIONS

1. Observe Isaiah 3:1-4:1, marking key words including *judge* with a red "J" and *My people* in a distinct way. Review why God is judging Israel's leaders.

2. How are judgments on the righteous and the wicked contrasted in verses 10-11? How does this encourage you to stand for the Lord?

3. What did you learn from marking My people? How are leaders described? What have they done to the people?

4. How are the daughters of Zion described?

5. How will the Lord judge these arrogant women? What price will they pay with the loss of so many men?

6. What ideas and behaviors do people admire in today's leaders (politicians, celebrities, reporters)?

7. What can happen to those who stand for morality in immoral cultures? Have you counted the cost of being a Christian? Do you know how to give a Scriptural defense for your faith?

8. Record a theme for Isaiah 3 on your **At A Glance** chart.

Prayer

Lord, I confess it's easier to stand with a crowd than against it, to be approved rather than rejected. But I want a heart like Yours – one that desires holiness and righteousness. Help me press on relying on the wisdom of Your Word and the power of Your Spirit so I'll be useful to You wherever you take me. Strengthen me when I'm tempted to succumb to the world's lure. In the name of Your perfect Son, Amen.

Life or Judgment?

SYNOPSIS

As we move into Isaiah 5 today, you'll notice a theme that recurs in Isaiah's message: God must judge Israel's sin. Isaiah repeatedly exposes the heart and actions of these rebellious people, warns of God's imminent judgment, and calls for repentance. As you revisit these topics, think about how relevant they are for you, the Church, and your culture.

QUESTIONS

1. Re-read Isaiah 3:16-4:1. Summarize the conduct and appearance of the women and how they will be judged.

2. How do women's standards and choices influence the moral path of society today?

3. Compare these observations with Lamentations 1:1-3. How great is Israel's fall?

4. According to 1 Timothy 2:9-10 what behaviors reveal a godly woman? Do your behavior, speech, and dress reveal godliness or worldliness?

5. Now read Isaiah 4:2-5:7 and mark key words. Mark *survivors of Israel* and its synonyms and add it to your key-word list. (Don't miss references like *he who is left, remnant, everyone who is recorded for life in Jerusalem.*)

6. When does in *that day* refer to? Review Isaiah 2:1-4.

7. What did you learn from marking survivors?

8. How will God cleanse Jerusalem? What will Zion look like?

9. What is the glory in Israel (v.5)? Look up John 1:1 and 14 and note what you learn about glory.

10. According to Chapter 5, how did the gardener prepare His vineyard? What did He expect?

11. What did the vineyard produce? How did the gardener deal with this?

12. What fruit does Israel produce according to verse 7?

13. How does Israel's lifestyle parallel your nation's? Do you think God will judge your nation as He did Israel?

TODAY'S TEXT
Isaiah 4:1-6; 5:1-7

Where's That Verse?

CROSS-REFERENCES

Isaiah 3:16-26

Leviticus 11:44

Psalm 18:28; 36:9

Lamentations 1:1-3

Ezekiel 16:46-50

John 1:1, 14

Romans 6:23

2 Corinthians 5:21

1 Timothy 2:9-10

Hebrews 4:15

Prayer
Father, our country's spiritual condition is so similar to that of the Israel Isaiah described. We deserve Your wrath, but we ask for Your mercy—that You poor out Your Spirit, regenerate Your people, open their minds to understand Your Word and repent of their sins. Begin this revival in the Church; purify Your people. In Jesus' precious and pure name I pray, Amen.

Woe to the Wicked!

Where's That Verse?

CROSS-REFERENCES

Psalm 119:104

Jeremiah 46:11

Daniel 11:32

Hosea 4:1-6

John 8:32

Ephesians 5:16

SYNOPSIS

What happens to the deceivers and seducers of the world? Not content to sin in isolation, they lure others to join them in lying, manipulating, and deceiving. Isaiah delivers a timely message to these corrupt men: "The holy God will show Himself holy in righteousness" (Isaiah 5:16).

QUESTIONS

1. Observe Isaiah 5:1-25, marking key words and asking 5W and H questions. Mark *woe* with a red cloud shaded brown and *therefore* with three red dots like a triangle to discover the conclusion the speaker is making. Also identify and mark *well-beloved*.

2. Why does the well-beloved let His vineyard be trampled?

3. What behavior does the first woe address (v.8)? What happens to those who sin this way?

4. What behavior does the second woe address (v.11)? What do these people ignore?

5. What did you learn from marking therefore in verses 13-14? What becomes evident about God when He judges, according to verse 16?

6. Read Hosea 4:1-6. How do these verses compare with your observations in Isaiah 5?

7. What do you learn from the final four woes given in verses 18-23?

8. Does anyone you know, including yourself, resemble these people?

9. What do these sins result in? Why (v. 24)? What is God's judgment (v. 25)?

10. Meditate on today's sobering message. How will you respond? Consider the warning in Ephesians 5:15-17 and the truth of Psalm 119:104.

Prayer
Lord, only Your people can stand firm in these last days. Though many profess Your name, so few really know You through Your Word. Teach me from Your truth how to discern intentions and not be lured away by lies. Make me a light to this wicked world, speaking forth your true Word. In the name of the One who is the truth I pray, Amen.

God's Presence in You

SYNOPSIS

Has God dealt with you as He dealt with Israel? Although some don't think the Old Testament is relevant, Romans 15:4 says these things were written for our instruction. Life application is the goal of inductive Bible study—knowing, believing, and walking in truth.

TODAY'S TEXT
Isaiah 2:8-12, 17, 22; 3:8

Where's That Verse?

CROSS-REFERENCES

Isaiah 1:1; 42:8
Exodus 19:1-6
Leviticus 26:14-19
Deuteronomy 8:11-14
John 15:16
Acts 17:28
Romans 15:4
1 Corinthians 6:19
Colossians 3:5
Hebrews 13:5-6
1 Peter 1:16
Revelation 1:6

QUESTIONS

1. Compare God's calling Israel with His calling the Church. Look up the following verses. Note who chooses, who's chosen, when, why (for what purpose), what the elect are freed from and how they live subsequently.
   a. Exodus 19:3-6
   b. John 15:16
   c. Revelation 1:6
   d. 1 Peter 1:15-16

2. In the wilderness Israel lived in the very presence of God – a cloud by day and fire by night. Read Leviticus 26:14-19 and discuss the relationship of pride to disobedience.

3. According to Isaiah 3:8 what did Israel rebel against?

4. How do pride and complacency creep into the chosen man's life? Analyze Deuteronomy 8:11-14. What is God warning against?

5. What does Colossians 3:5 say about greed?

6. A key repeated word in Isaiah is *pride*—mark it (including synonyms) with a red arrow pointing up. Also mark references to being *humbled* with an arrow pointing down.
   a. Isaiah 2:8-17
   b. Isaiah 5:15

7. Do you realize that believers live in the presence of God (1 Corinthians 6:19)? Do people see God in your life by the way you act, talk, live, and treat others?

8. Are you living a life set apart for God's purpose—freed from the slavery of sin and bearing good fruit for His kingdom?

Prayer
Father, I know You're always present (Psalm 139:1-10) yet I sometimes feel distant from You. When I walk my own way, my vision is clouded by circumstances and emotions— a slippery slope toward sin. Help me live by the Spirit and walk in righteousness. I pray in the name of Jesus, the Lord Our Righteousness, Amen.

Becoming God-Conscious

Where's That Verse?

CROSS-REFERENCES

Exodus 13:21-22; 40:17, 19, 29, 34-38

1 Samuel 4:21

1 Kings 8:10-11

Ezekiel 10:1-5, 18-19; 11:22-23; 43:1-4

Romans 8:4

1 Corinthians 6:19

Ephesians 4:30

Philippians 2:15

Hebrews 13:5-6

1 Thessalonians 5:19

Did You Know?

The prophet Ezekiel was a Levite who lived more than 90 years after Isaiah. The Babylonians took him and 10,000 others captive during their second siege of Jerusalem. Although he didn't serve in the temple, God gave him visions of a future temple and priesthood. The city of Babylon was located in today's Iraq.

SYNOPSIS

Can you imagine living in the presence of the Lord day and night as Israel did? How then could they reject and rebel against Him? Many Christians indwelt by the Spirit of God similarly suppress God's leading, missing opportunities to receive His blessing. What about you?

QUESTIONS

1. Today we'll observe God's presence among His people in several cross-references. Cross-references aid interpretation since God rarely says everything about a subject in one place.

   Look up Exodus 13:21-22. How did God lead Israel out of Egypt?

2. Now read Exodus 40:17-38 and mark the key phrase *just as the Lord had commanded Moses.* List everything you learn about the cloud of the Lord.

3. Describe God's presence when Solomon moved the Ark of the Covenant to the newly built temple in 1 Kings 8:10-11.

4. Review Isaiah 3:8-11. Why did God's presence ultimately depart from Israel?

5. Observe Ezekiel's vision of God's presence leaving Israel in Ezekiel 10:1-5, 18-19 and 11:22-23. Read the **Did You Know?** section for the historical context.

6. When will God's presence return and how will it appear? Look up Isaiah 4:2-5 and Ezekiel 43:1-4.

7. Read Ephesians 4:30 and 1 Thessalonians 5:19. If a believer's body is God's temple and dwelling place (1 Corinthians 6:19), how should believers live?

8. Are you living by the Spirit, "putting to death the deeds of the body?" (Romans 8:13) Does your life bring glory to Him?

9. Record a theme for Isaiah 4 on your **At A Glance** chart.

Prayer

Father, what an awesome privilege it is to live in Your holy presence! But God, I'm so weak—so quick to rebel and surrender to my flesh. Strengthen me by Your Spirit and Word so I can serve You and bring glory to Your name. Use me as an instrument of righteousness for the furtherance of the Kingdom. In Jesus' name, Amen.

The Holiness of God

SYNOPSIS

Do you ever look at the world around you—the immorality, scandals, corruption, foolishness—and give yourself a pat on the back? When we measure ourselves by mans' average performance, we come out looking pretty good. But can we be so confident standing before a holy God whose rule is perfection?

TODAY'S TEXT
Isaiah 5:24-30; 6:1-8

Where's That Verse?

CROSS-REFERENCES

Leviticus 6:9, 12-13; 26:18

2 Chronicles 26:1, 3-5, 15-20

Joel 3:10

Matthew 12:34

1 Corinthians 10:12

QUESTIONS

1. Read Isaiah 5:24-30, marking key words and the phrase ***distant nation*** and its pronouns (it, its).

2. Why is the Lord angry with His people and how will He judge them (vv. 24-25)?

3. Who will raise up the *distant nation* to judge Israel? How is it described?

4. What does this passage teach you about God's character with respect to His dealings with the sin of His people and the nations?

5. Now read Isaiah 6:1-8, marking time phrases with a green clock. (Although Scripture frequently uses time units, also look for words that specify event order like "then," "until," "after this," and "when".)

6. When did this event occur? What did Isaiah witness?

7. How did he react to God's holiness? How was he helped?

8. What did the Lord ask? Why do you think Isaiah responded as he did?

9. Read 2 Chronicles 26:1-21, asking the 5Ws and H about King Uzziah.

   a. When did he become king?

   b. What was his relationship with the Lord like?

   c. What great things did he accomplish during his reign? Who helped him?

   d. What happened when he "became strong?" (v.16)

   e. How did God judge his pride?

10. Have you, like Isaiah, seen the wickedness of your sin in light of God's holiness? Have you been proud, self-righteous, as Uzziah was?

11. Look up 2 Corinthians 5:21 and note how we obtain true righteousness.

12. Is the Lord prompting you to respond in any particular way to this program? If so, go humbly before Him now and submit to His will.

13. Record a theme for Isaiah 5 on your **At A Glance** chart.

Prayer

Lord, I confess that I have become comfortable with a mediocre faith and complacent walk before You. It's so easy to look at the world's darkness and feel superior. But when I gaze on Your holiness I'm ashamed. Thank You for Your Son Jesus Christ, who became sin for me so I might become righteous in Him. Renew in me a zeal and passion for holiness. In His name I pray, Amen.

Where's That Verse?

CROSS-REFERENCES

Genesis 1:2, 26; 11:6-7

2 Chronicles 26:18

Proverbs 30:1-4

Matthew 3:17

John 1:1-2; 2:4; 12:27-28, 35-41; 13:9; 14:9

Revelation 13:8

The Richness of His Glory

SYNOPSIS

"The whole earth is filled with His glory" (Isaiah 6:3). Have you paused lately from your frantic pace to take in God's glory? Have you seen His awesome presence in creation? How does this impact your perspective on life and what does it compel you to do? Today we'll examine Isaiah's first-hand account of coming face-to-face with the Lord.

QUESTIONS

1. Read Isaiah 6:1-10, reviewing your observations from the previous program. Summarize Isaiah's vision.

2. Contrast King Uzziah's (2 Chronicles 26:16-20) and Isaiah's reactions to coming into God's presence. How did God respond to each of them?

3. What does God ask in Isaiah 6:8? What does He tell Isaiah to say?

4. How will people respond to His message?

5. Why does God ask on behalf of "Us?" Who is He referring to? Look up the following verses and list your insights.
   a. Genesis 1:2
   b. Genesis 1:16
   c. Genesis 11:6-7
   d. John 1:1-2, 14
   e. Proverbs 30:1-4 (Note the reference to God's son)
   f. John 14:9

6. Now read John 12:27-28 and 35-45. Why does the author quote from Isaiah? Why did some people reject Jesus? (What did they reject?)

7. What do these verses in John reveal about the Trinity? According to verse 41, who did Isaiah see in his vision?

8. Once more, contrast Isaiah's response to God with the people's in John 12:42-43. Whose approval do you seek? Are you willing to speak God's message to others?

9. Have you like Isaiah seen your sin, repented, and embraced Jesus as your Savior? Break from your busyness and meditate on God's glory. Seek His perspective on life in the Word and learn there what He wants you to do.

Prayer
Father, I have allowed pressures and demands in my life to crowd out time with You. Help me re-focus on Your holy calling and glorious presence. Don't let earthly things blind me to Your will. Renew my mind; replenish my strength; revive my spirit. I ask for these things in the most precious name of Jesus, Amen.

When the Word Falls on Deaf Ears

SYNOPSIS

When you've truly tasted the goodness of God and understood the truth of His Word, it's impossible not to be changed. Jesus' disciples said "…we cannot stop speaking about what we have seen and heard" (Acts 4:20). But what a bitter reality to see His Word fall on deaf ears! What does the Lord teach about those who reject Him?

QUESTIONS

1. Read Isaiah 6:8-13 and mark time phrases and references to *the land.* How long did God tell Isaiah to preach His message?

2. What kind of judgment did Israel face? Review Isaiah 5:13 and 26-30.

3. What hope is offered in 6:13? In light of Isaiah's commission, do you think this encouraged him to persevere?

4. How does this relate to the Christian's call to share the Gospel? Read the parable of the sower in Mark 4:3-20.
   a. What do you learn about soil types in verses 4-8?
   b. What does good soil yield?
   c. What does the sower sow?
   d. What causes so many to fall away?
   e. Why did Jesus share this parable with His disciples?

5. What is the Christian's commission? Look up Matthew 28:19-20 and note Jesus' promise.

6. What does Matthew 7:13 and 21 teach about those who enter the kingdom of heaven? What do all true disciples ultimately do?

7. Record a theme for Isaiah 6 on your **At A Glance** chart.

Prayer
God, You have given me everything I need to stand firm in this world for the truth of Your Word and for Your calling on my life. Give me courage and discipline to use every resource (my talents, time, and money) to be a worker in the field. People are perishing around me and You've equipped me with the Message that saves. Help me give it as freely as You gave it to me. In the name of the Lord Jesus, Amen.

TODAY'S TEXT
Isaiah 6:8-13

Where's That Verse?

CROSS-REFERENCES

Isaiah 1:4, 11-13; 4:4; 5:13

Jonah 2:9

Matthew 7:14, 18-22; 28:19-20

Mark 4:3-12

Luke 2:22; 19:41

John 1:14

Acts 26:8

1 Corinthians 6:19

1 John 3:1

Did You Know?

Isaiah 6:13 mentions "burning" land. Jerusalem burned twice—when the Babylonians first captured it in 586 B.C. and later when the Romans destroyed it in 70 A.D.

Steadfast and Immovable

Where's That Verse?

CROSS-REFERENCES

Ezra 4:10

Isaiah 2:22

Jeremiah 1:12; 13:11

1 Corinthians 15:58

Hebrews 11:6

Did You Know?

Isaiah's son's Hebrew name "Shear-jashub" means "A remnant shall return."

SYNOPSIS

When terror strikes your heart where do you turn? Does your faith crumble or do you remain unshaken, trusting in the Lord? God promises to reward those who seek Him. Stand firm and He will bring you through the most crushing trials.

QUESTIONS

1. Read Isaiah 7:1-9, asking the 5 W and H questions. Note who's involved, what's happening and where. Consult your map for the locations mentioned and mark time phrases with a green clock.

2. Why is the king fearful? How are he and his people described?

3. What does God tell Isaiah to do? What's his message?

4. Who is he to take with him and for what purpose? Read the **Did You Know?** section for additional insight.

5. What will happen to the king's adversaries? What did you learn from marking the time phrase?

6. What does Isaiah warn the king about in verse 9?

7. What do you learn about God's sovereignty from this passage?

8. Look up Hebrews 11:6. How does this verse relate to your observations today?

9. First Corinthians 15:58 says "be steadfast, immovable, always about in the work of the Lord." Spend the remainder of your study time meditating on this truth. Evaluate how you respond to trials, seemingly hopeless situations, then ask God for unshakable faith.

Prayer
Father, Your Word says that many will fall away through temptations and trials, but those who hold fast to the Word and persevere will receive Your kingdom. Help me stand firm no matter what the cost or situation is so that I'll be among the remnant found faithful to You. Give me an unshakeable faith in Your plan. In Jesus' name, Amen.

A Sign for Deliverance

SYNOPSIS

The Word of God is like a mirror—when we look into it (I mean, really stare into it), we see our shortcomings staring right back at us! We see what needs to change for our lives to measure up to God's standard, but we also see the power we have in Christ to make those changes. God calls us to account—we can't blame our failures on circumstances or people. And He shows us who we are in Him and the pattern He has for us to follow in Christ.

Where's That Verse?

CROSS-REFERENCES

Isaiah 6:1

Deuteronomy 24:1

2 Chronicles 26:19-21

Matthew 1:18-25

Luke 2:49, 52

John 16:8

Romans 5:12

1 Corinthians 10:12

2 Corinthians 5:21

2 Kings 15, 16 and 17

QUESTIONS

1. Review Isaiah 7:1-9 noting main characters, then read 2 Kings 15:23-31, 37 and 16:1-5. What do you learn about each king and especially their relationship to God?

2. Who sent Rezin and Pekah against Judah? What did Ahaz do that deserved God's judgment?

3. Now read Isaiah 7:10-14. What does God tell Ahaz to ask for? In light of your observations of Ahaz's character, does his response to this seem genuine?

4. Look up 2 Kings 16:7-9. Who does Ahaz trust for deliverance?

5. Who does Isaiah address at this point? What sign will God give?

6. Who is "Immanuel?" (Mark *Immanuel* in a distinct way and add it to your list of key words.) Read Matthew 1:18-25 and list your observations about Him.

7. Why is the virgin birth so significant?
    a. Where does sin come from according to Romans 5:12?
    b. Was Jesus conceived in sin?
    c. What did He become on our behalf and why according to 2 Corinthians 5:21?

8. Romans 5:12 says death spread to all men through sin. Who can you trust for deliverance—yourself (e.g. good works or character)? Are the life, death, resurrection, and ascension of Jesus essential for salvation? Why?

Prayer
Lord, thank You for Your Son Jesus – the greatest revelation of Your love and plan for redemption. I believe He was tempted in the flesh just as I am but did not sin and that through this He became sin on my behalf and clothed me in His righteousness. Thank You for this salvation and the power of the Holy Spirit that enables me to walk in Your ways. In Jesus most precious name, Amen.

Wait on the Lord

TODAY'S TEXT

Isaiah 7:9, 14-25; 8:1-8

Where's That Verse?

CROSS-REFERENCES

Isaiah 2:22; 6:1-13

2 Kings 15:29; 16:9

Habakkuk 2:4

Romans 1:16-17; 10:17

Did You Know?

Why is the prophecy of the Messiah in Isaiah 7:14 inserted in Isaiah's word to Ahaz and the house of David? Remember, the prophet had just foretold the "shattering" of Ephraim so that it would no longer be a people. God reminds His people in this prophecy that He will continue to be with them and fulfill His promise to establish a king in the house of David.

SYNOPSIS

Throughout biblical history, God called many men to serve Him—Abraham, Joshua, David, Solomon, plus all those listed in the Hebrews 11 "Hall of Faith." But what about those who planned and tried to execute their own agendas? Hebrews 11:6 says "Without faith it is impossible to please Him…." Whose plan are you following?

QUESTIONS

1. Review God's plan to deliver Judah and His warning to Ahaz in Isaiah 7:3-9. Then read Isaiah 7:14-25 and 8:1-8, marking time phrases and geographical locations.

2. Who did Ahaz trust for deliverance (2 Kings 16:7)? Go back and mark references to *Assyria* in orange in Isaiah chapters 7-8.

3. What did Isaiah prophesy about this alliance?

4. Describe Israel's conditions during Assyria's captivity.

5. When will all this come to pass (Isaiah 7:15 and 8:4)? See the **Did You Know?** section.

6. Carefully re-read Isaiah 8:5-8, asking the 5Ws and H to interpret the text.
   a. What does "these people rejected the gently flowing waters of Shiloah" mean? What did they reject?
   b. Rezin and the son of Remaliah were dead within two years of their assault on Judah—an apparent victory. Who do you think the people rejoiced in—God or Ahaz? Why?
   c. How is Assyria described and how will it take Judah?

7. Although Ahaz's plan seemed to bring victory to his people, what did his rejection of God's plan result in? Can you see any parallels in your life? Are you suffering consequences from following your own paths? Have they brought pain and hardship on others as well?

8. Romans 1:17 says "The righteous man shall live by faith." Are you walking by faith or by sight?

9. Record a theme for Isaiah 7 on your **At A Glance** chart

Prayer
Lord, my attempts to fix troubled relationships and difficult situations have resulted in greater pain, but You promised that those who wait on You will find new strength and will not grow weary. I desperately need Your strength to endure trials and my own flesh! Help me walk by faith – trust Your plan for delivery, healing, and restoration. In Your mighty Son's name I pray, Amen.

A Spring of Living Waters

PROGRAM 19

SYNOPSIS

When you know disaster is on the horizon, how do you keep a peaceful heart? God promises strength, power, patience… everything you need to stand firm through the storms of life. As we look today at God's dealings with His unfaithful children, we'll analyze His instructions to the faithful remnant in their midst.

TODAY'S TEXT
Isaiah 8:6-14

 Where's That Verse?

CROSS-REFERENCES

Isaiah 6:1-8, 13; 7:3, 9,14, 20; 8:1

Psalms 12:6; 119:104

Jeremiah 2:13-19

Acts 20:29

Ephesians 4:14

QUESTIONS

1. Read Isaiah 8:5-14, marking key words and geographical locations. Who does God address in verse 9 and what does He say? What does this teach about His dealings with *the nations* and His people?

2. Look up Jeremiah 2:13-19, put a number by the two evils listed in verse 13, then answer the following questions:

   a. What's the contrast in verse 13 and what does it mean?

   b. How is the land described?

   c. Why has God judged His people?

   d. How does this passage compare with your observations of chapters 7-8?

3. Now read 2 Kings 16 for greater insight into the apostasies and wickedness Israel committed during Ahaz's reign. List some of the ways Ahaz and the people walked "according to the abominations of the nations."

4. What are God's instructions to Isaiah in Isaiah 8:11-13? How do these apply to your life today?

5. Compare depravity in Isaiah's day and today. Are you living as an "alien and stranger" (1 Peter 2:11) in this world – set apart for God's purpose?

6. Do you fear the calamities, oppressions, and hardships of life – or do you trust the living, holy God to be a sanctuary in the storms of life?

Prayer
Father, I take shelter in Your loving arms, knowing You are absolutely in control. You called me out of darkness to serve Your purposes—I trust that You will use every one of my circumstances for Your glory and my sanctification. Make my heart teachable so I can cling to the truths of Your Word in times of adversity. In Jesus' name, Your Word made flesh. Amen.

Where's That Verse?

CROSS-REFERENCES

Isaiah 2:22; 6:13; 7:3, 9, 14; 8:1

Proverbs 23:7

Amos 3:6

Zechariah 13:7

Luke 2:25-32

John 8:12; 17:17

Romans 12:2

2 Peter 1:4; 3:3-9, 11-14

Did You Know?

"Bind up [the testimony]" and "Seal" imply no additions.

Light in Darkness

SYNOPSIS

Are you walking in darkness, uncertain about the present and afraid of the future? Scientists, politicians, leaders, and media today all present bleak outlooks for the world and religious and spiritual advisers respond with conflicting advice. Where will you turn for truth, solace, and sanctuary?

QUESTIONS

1. Read Isaiah 8:11-22 and 9:1-2, 6, asking the 5 W and H questions. Also mark *testimony* and law with a purple book, shaded green.

2. How does God want Isaiah to walk among "this people" and regard Him?

3. Recall the political climate and spiritual conditions of Israel at this time. Why will the Lord be a snare and trap for them?

4. Who will Isaiah and his disciples wait for?

5. What did you learn from marking testimony and law? How can you know if you're hearing truth?

6. Who do the Israelites consult rather than God's Word? Who do people today turn to for answers?

7. How will God judge those who don't obey His Word?

8. What is the hope for those in darkness – what will they see and where? What do you learn about the coming ruler in 9:6?

9. Look up Luke 2:25-32 – the account of one of God's faithful. What was he waiting for? How does he describe Jesus?

10. Read 2 Peter 3:3-14. How should believers today wait on the Lord and why?

11. What source will you depend on to be found "spotless and blameless?" Read Christ's prayer for believers in John 17:17.

12. Add a theme for Isaiah 8 to your **At A Glance** chart.

Prayer
Lord, You promised Your followers that they will never walk in darkness. You are the light of life (John 8:12). Though everything around me crumbles, Your path for me is illuminated, so my soul is secure. Help me resist the voices of the world – its lies and schemes – that tempt me to depart from Your truth. Keep my heart at rest. In Jesus' name, Amen.

A Sign of Hope

SYNOPSIS

"**If you will not believe, you surely shall not last.**" Ahaz rejected Isaiah's sobering call to faith, proud and determined to follow his own plan. How many times have you done the same? Who rules your life?

QUESTIONS

1. Read Isaiah 7:14 (10-14 for context) and 9:6-7. Mark *sign* with an orange stop sign shaded yellow and *child* with a purple circle shaded yellow.

2. What sign will God give? What does His name mean?

3. What did you learn about this child? What will He do? For how long?

4. What did God promise David in 2 Samuel 7:8-16?

5. How is this sign a fulfillment of God's promise to David? Look up Matthew 1:1, 18-25 and note the lineage.

6. Who will the child "govern?" Read Isaiah 10:20-22, 11:10, and Romans 9:24-27.

7. While Isaiah 9:6-7 reaches to the far future, Jesus calls His people to follow Him today. What did He say to those who die rejecting Him in John 8:24? Read the Did You Know? section for additional insight.

8. Who is the ultimate authority in your life? Who rules relationships, parenting, the workplace, church service, etc.—Jesus or you?

Prayer

Father, I submit every area of my life to Your authority. Forgive the times I was faithless, thinking I controlled my circumstances and life. Thank You for Your grace and call on my life. I trust Your plan of hope and victory. In Jesus' name, Amen.

TODAY'S TEXT
Isaiah 9:6-7

Where's That Verse?

CROSS-REFERENCES

Isaiah 5:13; 7:2, 6, 9-14; 10:20-22; 11:1, 10

Exodus 3:14-15

2 Samuel 7:8-16

Psalms 119:104

Matthew 1:18-25

John 8:24

Romans 5:12

2 Corinthians 5:21

Ephesians 6:4

Colossians 2:13-14

Hebrews 11:6

 Did You Know?

In Exodus 3, The Lord says to Moses "I am who I am . . . . Thus you shall say to the sons of Israel. I Am has sent me to you" (Exodus 3:14). "I Am" is one of God's names: "My memorial-name to all generations" (Exodus 3:15).

A Great Light to Those in Darkness

TODAY'S TEXT
Isaiah 9:1-7

Where's That Verse?

CROSS-REFERENCES

Isaiah 7:9, 14; 8:13-14, 16, 19-22; 9:1-7

Matthew 4:12-17; 11:28-30

John 1:4, 9; 3:3, 5, 16-20; 9:5

Romans 8:37

Did You Know?

Zebulun and Naphtali were among the first tribes Assyria took captive (2 Kings 15:29).

SYNOPSIS

Are you walking in darkness, depression, and despondency? Overwhelmed with trials and opposition? Isaiah 9 prophesies the birth of a child who will break oppressors with a rod of iron and rule justly and mercifully on the throne of David, forever increasing His rule and peace.

QUESTIONS

1. Read Isaiah 8:19-22 and 9:1-7 in one sitting to learn how the chapters connect. How are the people described?

2. What will happen in the regions listed in verse 1? Who fulfills this prophecy according to Matthew 4:12-17?

3. What will God do for those who walk in darkness (9:2-5)?

4. Look up John 1:4, 9; 3:16-20, and 9:5. Who is the light and what do you learn about Him? Who rejects the light and why?

5. Review your list on the child in Isaiah 9:6-7. What do these descriptions tell you about Jesus' character as ruler and savior? Meditate on His names and what these attributes mean to you.

6. Consider the questions in the program introduction. What is the source of your darkness? Have you surrendered your life to Jesus? Has He freed you from the burden and bondage of sin? If not, ask God today for forgiveness of your sins and commit to following His Son Jesus. Read Jesus' promise in Matthew 11:28-30.

7. Do you need to submit once more to God's will and ask Him for joy and peace in the midst of a discouraging trial? Read Romans 8:35-39 to understand the depths of His unchanging, conquering love.

Prayer
Lord, You are truly wonderful – you sympathize with our weaknesses but you successfully resisted temptation and conquered death. You reveal Your Father's counsel and power. You give eternal life and peace to Your people. I thank You today for calling me out of darkness and making me a son of light. In the name of Your Son, the only true Light of the world, I pray, Amen.

His Righteous Anger

SYNOPSIS

Many people today reject God's righteous anger and judgments against sinners claiming that a "God of love" doesn't do such things. Are they right, or is God just, righteous, and holy?

QUESTIONS

1. Read Isaiah 9:5-21, marking key words from your bookmark. Also mark:
   a. *righteousness* with a blue R
   b. *therefore* with three red dots like a triangle
   c. *in spite of all this, His anger* with a red cloud, colored yellow
   d. *pride* with a brown arrow pointing up
   e. *time phrases*
   f. *geographical locations*

2. Note the subject shift in verse 8. Who's God warning now? Read the **Did You Know?** section for additional insight.

3. Examine each place you marked *therefore.* How do the people respond to God's judgment in verses 9-10? Verse 13? Verses 18-21?

4. Who will God raise up against them (vv.11-12)? What will they do?

5. Who will God cut off? Why? Compare this with Jeremiah 14:14.

6. How does the imagery in verses 18-21 describe the wickedness in Israel? What are they doing to one another and who are they against?

7. What does the repeated phrase *in spite of all this, His anger does not turn away* convey about God's displeasure with Israel? Why isn't His anger satisfied? What does this teach you about Him?

8. How can you apply this to your life? Hebrews 12 says God disciplines His children so they'll become holy. Has He disciplined you to perfect you?

9. Israel refused to repent, turn back to God. Have you submitted to God's judgment, confessed and repented from your sin?

10. Add a theme for Isaiah 9 to your **At A Glance** chart.

Prayer

Father, You discipline Your children because You love righteousness. Lord, make my heart teachable and receptive to Your judgments and discipline. Help me walk humbly before You, obedient to Your Word. I long for the peace only You can give. In Jesus' matchless name, Amen.

TODAY'S TEXT
Isaiah 9:5-19

Where's That Verse?

CROSS-REFERENCES

Isaiah 7:9, 25; 8:6-9

Ezekiel 13:9

Jeremiah 14:14

Luke 9:23

Mark 4:31-32

Galatians 2:20; 3:28-29

Did You Know?

Isaiah prophesied to the southern kingdom Judah (Jerusalem), while Hosea spoke God's word to the northern kingdom Israel, which was sometimes called by the largest tribe, "Ephraim." However, Isaiah often cites God's judgment on Israel to warn Judah.

In light of the split in the kingdom, when Isaiah says "The Lord sends a message against Jacob, and it falls on Israel" (Isaiah 9:8), "Jacob" may refer to the whole nation and "Israel" to the northern kingdom.

PROGRAM 24

TODAY'S TEXT
Isaiah 10:1-33; 11:1

Where's That Verse?

CROSS-REFERENCES

Isaiah 2:22; 5:24-25; 6:9-13; 7:3, 14; 9:6, 19-21

Hebrews 12:6-11

An Outstretched Hand

SYNOPSIS

Second Chronicles 28:22 says "in the time of his distress this same King Ahaz became yet more unfaithful to the Lord." How quickly we fall away in difficult times! Rather than trusting God, we tend to try to solve problems on our own. How do you handle adversity and conflict? What brings you to repentance?

QUESTIONS

1. Read Isaiah 10, marking key words from your bookmark and time phrases. Then carefully re-read the chapter, marking *Assyria* in orange and *remnant* in a distinct way. Include pronouns.

2. Who does God speak the first *woe* to in verse 1 and why? What does He warn them about?

3. What do you learn about *Assyria* in verses 5-6? What does this teach you about God's judgments?

4. What is Assyria's intention in oppressing Jerusalem? (v.7) How does Assyria's motive compare with God's?

5. What will the Lord do to Assyria when He finishes judging Jerusalem?

6. Who does Assyria credit its victories to? How will God humble their pride?

7. What did you learn about the remnant? Review what God says about them in Isaiah 6:9-13 and 7:3.

8. What hope does God give this faithful minority?

9. Who does God discipline and why according to Hebrews 12:6-11, and how have you responded to it?

10. In light of your study, will individuals and nations get away with cruelly oppressing widows and orphans? Does God care about the poor and helpless?

11. Record a theme for Isaiah 10 on your **At A Glance** chart.

Prayer
Lord, I want to be within *the remnant*—those who stand firm regardless of what happens to them. Help me respond well to Your discipline, Your reproof, Your "reproving" me. I know my heart is prone to wander and my wisdom to deceive me, but I want to be obedient. Mold me, mature me. In Jesus' name, Amen.

A Shoot from Jesse

SYNOPSIS

Do you ever wonder how an Old Testament book like Isaiah can be relevant to your life? Think about what you've seen of God's grace, justice, holiness, righteousness, and might. Because He's unchanging, God works the same ways today He did back then: He always judges sin and He always keeps a faithful remnant for Himself.

QUESTIONS

1. Today we'll conclude the second segment of Isaiah (chapters 7-12). Read Isaiah 11:1-16 and 12:1-6, marking key words from your bookmark. Note everything you learn from marking the following:
   a. *Knowledge* (dark green)
   b. *Righteousness* (blue R)
   c. *Then* (green circle)
   d. Time phrases like *in that day*
   e. *Remnant*
   f. *Salvation* (with a large S)
   g. Geographical locations including *in all the earth*
2. How is the Messiah described in Isaiah 11:1-5? What do you learn about His righteousness?
3. Look up Revelation 22:16-17 and read the **Did You Know?** section for additional insight into the identity of the Messiah.
4. Compare Isaiah 11:4 with Revelation 19:15-16. What do you learn about His judgment?
5. How is His kingdom described in Isaiah 11:6-10?
6. What do you observe about *knowledge* in verse 9? How does this contrast with the condition of God's people described in Isaiah 5:13 and Hosea 4:6?
7. Now list your observations on the Messiah's dealings with the nations and remnant. What will happen to each?
8. Read Zechariah 13:8-9 and Matthew 24:31 for additional insight into the remnant.
9. What will the *remnant* understand about God and who will they tell, according to Isaiah 12? What did you learn from marking *salvation*?
10. Review names you studied in this segment of Isaiah: *Immanuel* (God with Us), *Maher-shalal-hash-baz* (Swift is the booty, speedy is the prey), and Shear-jashub (a remnant will return). How are these names realized in Isaiah 12?
11. Record a theme for Isaiah 11 on your **At A Glance** chart.
12. Are you waiting to enter God's glorious resting place? Do you realize that you can experience His strength and peace even now as you await Jesus' return? Have you tasted waters "from the springs of salvation?" Call on His name today.

Prayer
Father God, I am thankful to live at a time in history when Your Word has been fully revealed and Your Son made known. I lay down my burdens and problems at His feet and ask Him to rule my life with His grace. Help me abide in You to bear fruit. May the joy, peace, and love You have poured into my heart overflow to those around me. In Jesus' name, Amen.

TODAY'S TEXT
Isaiah 11:1-16; 12:1-6

Where's That Verse?

CROSS-REFERENCES

Isaiah 5:13; 6:13, 7:9, 14; 9:6-7

Genesis 3:15; 49:10

Hosea 4:6

Zechariah 13:8-9

Matthew 24:31

John 1:3; 14:17, 20

Hebrews 4:9-10

Revelation 1:8; 19:15-16; 22:16-17

Did You Know?

The Messiah is "the shoot" from David "the stem" (son) of Jesse. Read Matthew 1:1-17 to see Jesus' genealogy from Abraham.

Jesus came first to be the suffering Servant. He will return to judge the living and the dead.

The Oracles to the Nations

TODAY'S TEXT
Isaiah 13:1-6

Where's That Verse?

CROSS-REFERENCES

Isaiah 1:1; 2:2; 4; 6:1, 5-11; 7:1, 4, 9; 8:19-20; 9:6-7; 11:10; 14:28-29; 15:1; 17:1

Amos 3:7

Ephesians 4:14

Did You Know?

From 729 B.C. Babylon was part of the Assyrian Empire. The ruler of Assyria assumed the title "King of Babylon." Babylon then became the capital of the Neo-Babylonian Empire which Nebuchadnezzar ruled after the death of his father, Nabopolassar. Nebuchadnezzar first besieged Jerusalem in 605 B.C. In 586 B.C. he destroyed Jerusalem and the temple.

Babylon was located in the territory that is now Iraq.

SYNOPSIS

How will God deal with men who don't believe in Him? Will He hold them accountable for sin? We have examined God's judgment of His people. Now, as we enter this next section in Isaiah, you will see God's sovereignty over nations and individuals.

QUESTIONS

1. Review your **At A Glance** chart and consider the main points of the first two sections you studied. What are the overall themes of chapters 1-6 and 7-12?

2. Today we will begin a new segment in Isaiah, chapters 13-23: "The Oracles to the Nations." Read chapter 13:1-6, marking key words including references to God's *anger* and time phrases.

3. Who does this first oracle concern? Mark references to this nation and its king in black, with a purple "B." Read the **Did You Know?** section for more information about this country. Also, locate it on your map and note its proximity to Jerusalem.

4. What do you learn about God's sovereign judgment in verses 2-3?

5. What does God command His "consecrated ones" and "mighty warriors" to do in verse 3? How will it happen?

6. How does God refer to this group in verse 5 and what do you learn about them? How vast is the destruction?

7. Cyrus the Great and Darius the Mede defeated the Babylonian Empire in 539 b.c. (though they did not destroy the city). Does this prophecy reach beyond this? What phrase helps you understand this?

8. Oracles are sometimes called "burdens" because they pronounce coming judgments. How does God hold these nations accountable for their disbelief and sin?

9. What about atheists, agnostics, and worshipers of other gods today? In light of what you've learned about God in Isaiah, how will God deal with these people?

10. "Consecrated" means set apart for a special purpose. What does God want you to do to people around you? Do you effectively communicate His truth to them – present them with light and life?

11. Read 2 Thessalonians 1:7-9 and list what happens to those who don't know God and disobey His Gospel. What does this truth compel you to do?

Prayer
Lord, Your Word says You made Yourself evident to all men so that all are without excuse (Romans 1:18-19). And You call Your people to sound forth Your Word. Use me, Lord, to speak the saving knowledge of Jesus Christ to others. Make me diligently study the scriptures so I can be prepared at all times to answer for the hope within me. In Jesus' name, Amen.

The Day of His Burning Anger

SYNOPSIS

Do you ever look at society and wonder where man's shame has gone? How can people do the things they do and say the things they say with such boldness, with no fear of God? An awesome and horrible day is coming when men who have done what is right in their own eyes will discover the Holy God.

QUESTIONS

1. Observe Isaiah 13:5-16, marking key words from your bookmark. Mark the **Lord,** His anger, and **destruction.** Add the day of the Lord to your list of key words and mark it with an orange box shaded pink. Look for geographical references like **world, earth,** and **land.**

   Suggestion: when you have a large list of key words, mark two or three at a time, asking the 5 Ws and H as you read. You don't want to miss the meaning of the passage. Repetitive reading will help you memorize the scriptures.

2. How will men react to *the day of the Lord?*

3. What kind of people face God's wrath? What happens to them?

4. Does this help you understand God's purpose for this day? What is it?

5. What will happen to the land? (Define the land from the context.) How will this event impact the heavens and earth?

6. What did you learn about the Lord from this passage? What do you learn about His holiness, judgment on sin, sovereignty, etc.?

7. Now look up Joel 2:1-12 and mark references to the day of the Lord. Compare your observations with Isaiah 13 as you answer the following:
   a. Where is this warning given?
   b. How is *the day of the Lord* described?
   c. How is God's army described?
   d. What does the Lord say in verse 12? What does this tell you about Him?

8. Read Malachi 4:5-6. What happens before the day of the Lord and to those with unrepentant hearts on it?

9. Does understanding this "day" affect you? Is God calling you to repent of something or call others to repentance?

10. Lastly, read Romans 1:21-32—a commentary on man's moral decay. What have men "exchanged" and for what? What has God given them over to? What are all these things "worthy of"?

TODAY'S TEXT
Isaiah 13:1, 4-16

 Where's That Verse?

CROSS-REFERENCES

Isaiah 1:2

Numbers 32:23

Psalm 51:5

Joel 2:1-12

Malachi 4:5-6

John 3:19

Romans 1:21-32

Revelation 11:3-8

Prayer
Lord, I so admire the Gentile woman's humility, boldness, and faith. May I pursue You with equal passion and persistence. Grant me the wisdom, faith, and understanding to recognize truth from error as well as the signs of Your coming. Amen.

TODAY'S TEXT

Isaiah 13:8, 11, 13, 17-22

Where's That Verse?

CROSS-REFERENCES

Malachi 4:5-6

Matthew 3:7

1 Thessalonians 5:1-2

2 Thessalonians 2:2-3

1 Peter 1:16

Revelation 17:1-6, 15-18; 18:4-5, 8, 10, 20, 2312

Did You Know?

The Medes and Persians defeated Babylon in 539 B.C. but God foretells a more extensive judgment on Babylon in Revelation.

"Babylon is fallen!"

SYNOPSIS

It's easy to get caught up in day-to-day life and miss what's going on around the world. But God revealed specific future events to His prophets to give hope to His children and warning to the world. Are you tuned it? Are you prepared?

QUESTIONS

1. Review your Isaiah 13:1-16 observations and then read verses 17-22, marking key words. Who will God send against Babylon?

2. What will they do to Babylon's people? What do you learn about future generations?

3. How will the land look after this devastation? Read the **Did You Know?** section for additional insight.

4. Observe Revelation 17:1-6, 15-18, asking the 5 Ws and H about the harlot.
   a. Who is she?
   b. What is her relationship to the world?
   c. What does she do to the Lord's people?
   d. How will she be judged and by whom?

5. Continue your observations of the harlot in Revelation 18:1-5, 8-10, and 20.
   a. How is she described?
   b. What do you learn about the nations?
   c. What warning does God give His people?
   d. How is the harlot judged?
   e. Why does God pronounce judgment on her?

6. Look up the following verses and note what you learn about the day to come.
   a. 1 Thessalonians 5:1-3
   b. 2 Thessalonians 2:3

7. How can you apply these prophecies and warnings to your life? What do you have to know to stand firm?

8. Record a theme for Isaiah 13 on your **At A Glance** chart.

Prayer
Lord, create in me a desire to know the Word so I will not be shaken when testing and tribulation come. These prophecies seem so surreal, so impossible. But Jesus said we need to be ready for His return and only the Bible's truth will strengthen us to endure until the end. Come quickly, Lord Jesus. In Your mighty name, Amen.

Life After Death

SYNOPSIS

Is there life after death? When the body dies, does the soul cease to exist? Philosophers, theologians, and scientists have debated this age-old question through the millennia . . . but only God's Word answers it.

QUESTIONS

1. Observe Isaiah 14:1-16 and mark references to Babylon and its king. Look carefully for time phrases and geographical locations. If the land refers to Israel (Canaan or land of the Lord), double underline it in green and shade it blue.

2. What do you learn about the Lord in verses 1-5? What will He do for Israel and to Babylon?

3. What will Israel do to the peoples in their midst (v.2)?

4. Analyze the taunt against the King of Babylon. What do you learn about this oppressor? How does he rule and how does the earth respond to his defeat?

5. How is he humbled –how invincible did he think he was?

6. Mark references to *Sheol* (the transliterated Hebrew; hell and hades in other versions) with a red S in verses 11-15. What is it like, where is it, and who is there?

7. What do the kings of other nations say to Babylon's king?

8. If someone asks you about the afterlife, what can you tell them based on your observations today?

9. Will anyone escape judgment? (Consider the world's worst criminals.)

TODAY'S TEXT
Isaiah 14:1-16

Where's That Verse?

CROSS-REFERENCES

Isaiah 2:22

Numbers 32:23

Psalm 119:104

Mark 9:44

Luke 16:26

John 14:6; 16:8-9

Romans 1:11

2 Corinthians 5:21

2 Peter 1:21

Revelation 17:4-6; 18:2; 20:12-14

Prayer

Oh Father, thank you for Your Son Jesus—the way, the truth, and the life. You sent Him to die for me so I can be cleansed from sin and spend eternity with You. Use my faith to bring those separated from You, lost in sin and deception, to this knowledge and freedom. Add grace to my speech and soften their hearts to receive Your Word. I pray in Jesus' name, Amen.

Who Can Turn Back His Hand?

Where's That Verse?

CROSS-REFERENCES

Isaiah 13:2

Genesis 11:1-9

Numbers 32:23

Psalm 139:9; 11

Jeremiah 50:1-3; 51:53

Luke 16:19-31; 23:42-43

1 Corinthians 15:20

2 Corinthians 5:8

Colossians 1:18

Revelation 20:7-14

Did You Know?

Marduk and Bel were Babylonian deities. Bel was the Babylonian equivalent of Baal.

SYNOPSIS

History is full of leaders who oppressed nations the way Babylon's king did, other kings whose unrestrained persecutions "made the earth tremble." But how did they end up? Like every man who chooses to be his own god, judgment and death!

QUESTIONS

1. Read Isaiah 14:1-15 for context and then observe verses 16-27, marking key words including references to **Babylon** and its king, time phrases, and geographical locations.

2. Describe the king of Babylon's descent. How far did he fall?

3. What will the Lord do to Babylon's people and land, according to verses 22-23?

4. How do Jeremiah 50:1-3 and 51:53 compare with Isaiah 13-14? Read the **Did You Know?** section for additional insights.

5. What attribute of God is described in Isaiah 14:24-27?

6. What does this teach you about His plan for your life? Can circumstances, people, or even sin stop His plan for you?

7. Look up Psalm 139:7-11. Does God simply overlook good and evil? What then can you can conclude about judgment?

8. Where do the wicked go after death? Carefully read Luke 16:19-31 and answer the following questions.
   a. What happened to the two men after they died?
   b. Where are they? (Note every detail.)
   c. What does the rich man ask for?
   d. What does *not* persuade repentance according to Abraham?

9. Is Hades the final destiny? Read Revelation 20:13-14 and list who is judged, how, and what happens to them.

10. Now look up Luke 23:42-43 (read 39-41 for context) and 2 Corinthians 5:8. What happens to believers after they die?

11. Reflect on your walk with Christ. Does today's program give you assurance and hope? Do you fear judgment because you've been walking your own way, filling the desires of your flesh?

Prayer

Lord, I'm so grateful You're in control—nothing can hinder Your plan! You called me to Yourself and promised to complete the work You began in me. Help me walk in righteousness so I have no doubt, no fear of judgment. Make me hear and obey Your voice so I won't lose sight of the prize in heaven awaiting me. In Jesus' victorious name I pray, Amen.

Refuge in the Lord

SYNOPSIS

When your world has collapsed and your hope seems shot, what can you say to those around you? Can our faith be completely destroyed? Or do we always have the opportunity to return to the rock of our salvation, the immovable sovereign God, who promises refuge and strength to the afflicted who turn to Him?

QUESTIONS

1. Observe Isaiah 14:28-32, marking time phrases with a green clock and God in yellow. Mark **crying** (*wail, mourn*) with a blue teardrop.

2. Who does this oracle concern and when did it occur?

3. What does God warn Philistia of in verse 29?

4. What will He do for the "helpless" and "needy" in Israel? Think about what brought them to this state.

5. What two things will God use to judge Philistia?

6. How is this nation from the north described?

7. The messengers in verse 32 inquire about Israel. How will Israel answer them about Jerusalem's welfare?

8. What is the significance of Zion? Review what happens there in the last days according to Isaiah 2:1-3.

9. Consider the questions in the introduction. Are you confident the Lord can sustain you through tribulations and trials? Even if God has judged you for your sins, will you return to Him in Zion to receive truth and comfort from His Word?

Prayer
Lord, when the world threatens to overwhelm me, You are there to provide rest and refuge. All I can do is surrender my hurt, my disappointments, my grief to You and trust You to carry me through the storm. Restore peace to my heart and strengthen my faith for what lies ahead. In Jesus' name, Amen.

PROGRAM 31

TODAY'S TEXT
Isaiah 14:28-32

Where's That Verse?

CROSS-REFERENCES
Isaiah 2:1-3; 6:1; 8:4

Exodus 7:10-12

1 Samuel 4:1; 5:1-4

Psalm 30:5

John 16:33

Did You Know?

The Egyptian and Hebrew word for "Philistines," plishah, means "invasion."

The Philistines' origin is basically unknown. Egyptian records suggest they were part of a larger movement of sea peoples from the Aegean Sea that lines Greece. They settled in Cyprus and came down to attack Egypt, but Ramses III beat them back. They moved east from Egypt, fought the Hittites, and ended up in northern Syria. They continued to move toward modern-day Gaza on the coastline of the Mediterranean Sea. They were the source of the name "Palestine." Roman Emperor Hadrian changed "Judea" to "Syria-Palestine" (a sub-province of Syria). Later this was shortened to "Palestine."

Scholars are not sure whether the "the rod" in verse 29 is Assyria or Judah.

His Dwelling Place

TODAY'S TEXT
Isaiah 14:29, 32

Where's That Verse?

CROSS-REFERENCES

Leviticus 25:2, 23

Deuteronomy 12:5

2 Samuel 5:7

2 Chronicles 6:5-6, 10, 24-25, 28-31; 7:14

Psalms 2:1-6, 10-12; 18:2; 30:5; 46:1

Proverbs 18:10

2 Peter 1:19

Revelation 5:10; 13:8; 21:2, 4

SYNOPSIS

God knows all your sins and their consequences—your pain, failures, disappointments, and trials—and He plans to end both. He has prepared a place where there will be no more sin, tears, sorrow, pain or death. Call to Him, run to His presence, and "the joy of the Lord will be your strength."

QUESTIONS

1. Review Isaiah 14:28-32. What do you learn about Zion (Jerusalem)?

2. In Leviticus 25 the Lord gives Moses the statutes concerning the land of Israel. What do you learn about the land in verse 23? Who owns it?

3. Look up Deuteronomy 12:5 (verses 1-11 for context). Where will God establish His name? What will the people do there?

4. What do you learn about Zion from 2 Samuel 5:7?

5. Read 2 Chronicles 6:5-6, 10 (verses 1-17 for context), listing your observations about God's house.

6. Now read 2 Chronicles 6:20-33. What does Solomon ask the Lord to do for His people? Where? What does he request for the foreigner and why?

7. How does God answer Solomon? Read 2 Chronicles 7:12-16.

8. Finally, read Psalm 2. Note what the text says about Zion, the nations, and God's warnings in verses 10-12.

9. In light of your study, does the mercy in Isaiah 14:32 extend to Philistia as well?

10. "How blessed are all who take refuge in Him!" (Psalm 2:12) Are you seeking God in the midst of your trials? Are you resting in His promises to be your help, strength, and shield?

11. Record a theme for Isaiah 14 on your **At A Glance** chart.

Prayer
Lord, just as You chose Zion to be Your dwelling place, You chose to indwell Your Church through Your Holy Spirit. I know You're always with me, but stresses and difficulties make You seem so distant. Draw me close to You; renew the joy of my salvation and the hope of glory. In Jesus' name, Amen.

A Prideful Nation's Ruin

SYNOPSIS

When a man is stripped of everything, what causes him to harden his heart and shake his fist at God? Pride! Today, we'll examine the fate and choices of an arrogant nation that fell under God's wrath.

QUESTIONS

1. Observe Isaiah 15:1-9 and 16:1-5. Mark key words, especially references to *wailing (crying)* with a blue teardrop. Also note the nation's location and its proximity to Jerusalem on your map.

2. What country does God address this oracle to and what has happened to it?

3. Why are the people crying? Note who is wailing and other descriptions of their grief. Also find out where they go to weep.

4. How are the land and waters described? What has happened to them?

5. What will God to this nation according to verse 9?

6. What is the instruction to this nation in 16:1?

7. What do they request in 16:3-4a? What will the refugees find in Israel?

8. Read the following cross-references and note everything you learn about Zion.
   a. Psalm 9:11-20
   b. Psalm 481-3, 8
   c. Zechariah 8:2-3, 6-8

9. What does the Moabite outcast seeking refuge in Israel have to be willing to do, to surrender?

10. What kind of ruler will one day reign over the people in Zion? Why does the Lord place this Messianic promise in the oracle to Moab?

11. How can you apply this oracle to your life? Are you willing to lay down your pride and seek refuge in God in the day of distress? Or like Moab, will you turn to people and things to give you a false sense of security?

12. Are you willing to be refuge to others… even your enemies?

Prayer

Father, Moab is like so many I know—unwilling to surrender their pride, seeking salvation in the gods of this world, and weeping in their utter hopelessness. Lord, use this passage to remind me to walk humbly before You and be a light on the hill to others who are desperately searching for truth and relief. In Jesus' holy name, Amen.

TODAY'S TEXT
Isaiah 15:1-9; 16:1-5

Where's That Verse?

CROSS-REFERENCES
Genesis 12:3; 19:24-26, 37-38
Psalm 9:11-14; 30:5; 48:1-3, 8
Jonah 3:5
Zechariah 8:2-3, 6-8

Did You Know?

Tribute: a payment made to a foreign ruler as a sign of submission or non-citizenship. (Achtemeier, Paul J., Harper's Bible Dictionary. 1st ed. San Francisco: Harper & Row, 1985, p. 1097)

Moab: a narrow strip of land directly east of the Dead (Salt) Sea. Its inhabitants, Moabites, were neighbors to the Israelites. Moab, the father of the Moabites, was Lot's son by his firstborn daughter. Moab conflicted with Israel and even enslaved it at one point in history. Ancient Moab was part of what is now Jordan.

God Opposes the Proud

TODAY'S TEXT

Isaiah 16:1, 5-12

Where's That Verse?

CROSS-REFERENCES

Isaiah 14:13-15

Genesis 3:5; 19:30-38

Did You Know?

Some scholars believe the prophecy of Moab's judgment in verses 13-14 comes three years later, rather than recapping verses 1-12.

SYNOPSIS

Why is pride so deadly, so poisonous to heart and mind? Because it's the root and beginning of all sin. Pride convinced Adam and Eve to eat the fruit to be like God and many more have yielded to its subtle lure. How can you avoid this downfall?

QUESTIONS

1. Re-read Isaiah 15:1-9 and 16:1-5 for context. Then observe Isaiah 16:6-14, marking *wail* with a blue teardrop, *pride* with a red arrow pointing up, and *therefore.*

2. Describe Moab's *pride?*

3. What will happen to them? What will their enemies do to the land?

4. What do you learn about God from these verses? Especially note what He says in verses 9-10.

5. Who does Moab turn to in their crisis according to verse 12? How does this contrast with the refuge they could receive from Israel (16:3-5)?

6. What do you learn from verses 13 and 14? Read the **Did You Know?** section for additional information.

7. Record themes for chapters 15 and 16 on your **At A Glance** chart.

8. Read the following verses and list your observations about pride.
   a. James 4:6
   b. 1 John 2:15-17

9. Consider the questions in the introduction and evaluate your life in light of your study today. How can you avoid pride? What areas tempt you most and are you willing to humble yourself before God and others? What happens if you don't?

Prayer

Father, make me sensitive to Your Spirit and help me remember Your commands. I want to live according to the Word, but sometimes I lean on my own understanding and follow my own path. The world says I can "have it my way," but clearly from Moab's example this comes at a high cost. Keep my eyes fixed on You; help me stay the course. In Jesus' name, Amen.

Men and the Maker

SYNOPSIS

It's interesting how some people grade sins to make themselves feel more righteous than others. As we look at another wicked and idolatrous nation facing God's judgment, consider the following sins listed in Colossians: immorality, impurity, passion, evil desire, and greed. Have you dabbled in any of these areas?

QUESTIONS

1. Read Isaiah 17 and 18 slowly, paying attention to the vivid imagery in this oracle. Mark time phrases with a green clock and identify the different nations. Read the **Did You Know?** section for additional information.

2. Who's facing judgment in verses 1-3 and who are they compared to in verse 3? What happens?

3. Who does the subject shift to in verse 4? What will happen to them and their land?

4. What will God's judgment cause the people to do according to verse 7?

5. What do you learn about their behavior from verses 9-11? What will they suffer, according to verse 11?

6. Now what group in verses 12-14 will be judged? Although God used them to judge *Israel's* sin, what does this show you about God's faithfulness to His people?

7. What do you learn about the people of Cush in 18:1-2?

8. The "spreading branches" in verse 5 likely refers to Assyria, which conquered many nations including Israel and Damascus. What happens to these branches according to verses 5 and 6?

9. What will the "people tall and smooth" do following Assyria's judgment? Where do they go?

10. Record themes for chapters 17 and 18 on your **At A Glance** chart.

11. Do you "regard" the Lord Your Maker? Are you looking for His approval or the world's? Or have you forgotten the God of your salvation, the rock of your refuge?

12. Do you flirt with idols that bring on God's wrath (Colossians 3:5-6)?

Prayer

Lord, help me walk in the true knowledge of You. Self-proclaiming "men of God" preach things that tickle ears and entice flesh with prosperity, perfect health, no trials or sorrows. Give me strength to keep seeking the things above, knowing my reward is secure with You. In Jesus' name, Amen.

TODAY'S TEXT

Isaiah 17:1-14; 18:1-7

Where's That Verse?

CROSS-REFERENCES

Isaiah 7:4, 9; 14:29-32; 15:1

Psalm 30:5

Proverbs 18:10

Hosea 4:6

Matthew 25:31

Colossians 3:5

1 Peter 4:17

Did You Know?

Damascus is the oldest continually inhabited city in the world. It was a minor town until taken by the Arameans, a semi-nomadic people from the Arabian Peninsula that migrated into the region (modern-day Syria). According to Isaiah 7, the Arameans joined forces with Ephraim to attack the house of David under King Ahaz.

Don't forget: references to Jacob and Ephraim are synonymous with the Northern Kingdom of Israel.

Scholars believe Cush was located south of Egypt, the region today that includes Sudan, Ethiopia, and Somalia.

PROGRAM 36

TODAY'S TEXT
Isaiah 19:1-4, 12, 17

Where's That Verse?

CROSS-REFERENCES
Isaiah 14:24-27

Esther 4:14

Daniel 4:35

1 Corinthians 15:58

God's Purpose for the Nations

SYNOPSIS

Do you ever wonder if God is in control? Our society is crumbling morally; the political climate is a mess, and people are generally behaving very selfishly. An overall feeling of confusion seems to rest on the land. Is God orchestrating these events and what should the believer do during this time of uncertainty?

QUESTIONS

1. Observe Isaiah 19:1-4, 12 and 17 watching for what God does. Who does the oracle concern?

2. Who do the Egyptians worship according to verse 1?

3. What will the Lord cause to happen (v. 2)?

4. Who will the Egyptians turn to as their society crumbles? How does this compare to modern countries in times of hardship?

5. Who will God appoint to rule over them?

6. What word is repeated in verses 12 and 17? Compare these verses with Isaiah 14:24-27 and Daniel 4:35. What do all these verses teach about God?

7. If God has a purpose and is sovereign over the world, what can you conclude about your nation's current events? About your circumstances?

8. Can an evil person gain political control of a nation? Can he act outside of God's will?

9. Does uncertainty and confusion rattle your faith? What truths enable you to stand firm and trust God?

10. What does 1 Corinthians 15:58 command believers? How can you apply this to your life today?

Prayer
Lord, I place my trust in Your character that has endured throughout the ages: You are sovereign, ruler of heaven and earth, the omnipotent God. Help me stand firm in these times of confusion and upheaval and hold to the truths of Your Word. "Now may our Lord Jesus Christ Himself and God our Father, who has loved us and given us eternal comfort and good hope by grace, comfort and strengthen [our] hearts in every good work and word" (2 Thessalonians 2:16-17). Amen!

His Powerful Purpose

SYNOPSIS

Where can we find meaning in hardships and tragedies? How can understanding God's purposes and seeing how He worked in the past help me walk through life today? As you observe His works in today's program, think about His power, control, and involvement in life's details.

QUESTIONS

1. Read Isaiah 19 and color references to the *Lord* in yellow. Mark the time phrase *in that day* in a distinct way. Also mark *purpose(d)* with a squiggly line.

2. Review your observations on verses 1-4 from the last program – God's judgment on Egypt. How will this judgment impact daily life in Egypt according to verses 5-10?
   a. Mark references to *dry* and its synonym *parched.* What dries up?
   b. What industries are directly affected?
   c. How do the workers react? (Use words from the text.)

3. What do you learn about Egypt's leaders in verses 11-15? (Remember Egypt is historically renowned for its advanced technology and philosophies.) What has the Lord done to them and how has their leadership affected the people?

4. In verses 16-25 the phrase *in that day* is used six times.
   a. How are the Egyptians described in verse 16 and what has brought them to this state? Who will they dread and why?
   b. What else will happen "in that day" according to verse 18?
   c. Contrast the state of Egypt in verses 19-20 and verse 3. What have they built and where? Who will they turn to in their demoralized state this time? Who is their oppressor and who will deliver them?
   d. What do you learn from verses 21 and 22 about the Egyptians and the Lord? How do you know their vows to the Lord are genuine?
   e. As a result of the Egyptian's faith in the Lord, what will happen in that region of the world according to verses 23-25?

5. What was God's purpose for judging Egypt? Was their suffering in vain? What will He accomplish?

6. The Lord used a decaying society, failing government, declining economy, and oppressive regime to draw Egypt to Himself. What is He using in your life to draw you close? Who is your Deliverer?

7. James 1:12 says "Blessed is the man who perseveres under trial... He will receive the crown of life, which the Lord has promised to those who love Him." Ask God for the strength to endure and the faith to trust His purpose even when you don't understand it.

8. Record a theme for Isaiah 19 on your **At A Glance** chart.

Prayer
Lord, I am so blessed to be Your workmanship and inheritance in Christ. Like Egypt, draw me ever closer so I faithfully perform Your holy calling on my life. When trials test my faith, help me persevere and bring glory to Your name. In the name of your perfect Son I ask for these things. Amen.

TODAY'S TEXT

Isaiah 19:1-25

Where's That Verse?

CROSS-REFERENCES

Isaiah 14:24

1 Chronicles 12:32

Jeremiah 17:14

Daniel 11:36, 40-43

2 Corinthians 10:5

1 Timothy 2:2

PROGRAM 38

TODAY'S TEXT

Isaiah 20:1-6; 21:1-5

Where's That Verse?

CROSS-REFERENCES

Isaiah 14:24, 28; 19:22; 45:5-7

Jeremiah 29:11

Amos 3:6-7

Romans 8:28

2 Corinthians 3:18; 4:17-18

Did You Know?

The events in Isaiah 20 occur around 711 B.C.

Many scholars believe "the wilderness of the sea" is the modern-day Persian Gulf region.

Some commentators believe Israel looked to Merodach Baladan (Marduk-apal-addina) of Babylon to deliver them from the Assyrian king Sennacherib. But Assyria conquered Baladan, to their dismay and frustration.

"I Am God... There Is No Other"

SYNOPSIS

"The righteous man shall live by faith" (Romans 1:17). Trusting God in adversity means believing His promises rather than trying to solve problems on our own. As we continue our study today, ask the Lord for an immovable faith and vision of eternity.

QUESTIONS

1. Observe Isaiah 20, marking key words and time phrases; mark *sign* with an orange stop sign. Ask 5 W and H questions: who is this prophecy about, when was it given, what is going to happen, etc.

2. What did the Lord tell Isaiah to do? Why?

3. Who will be "dismayed and ashamed"?

4. Why were God's people putting their hope in these nations?

5. Record a theme for Isaiah 20 on your **At A Glance** chart.

6. Now observe Isaiah 21:1-5. How does Isaiah describe his vision? Read the **Did You Know?** section for the historical context.

7. In light of the historical context, why is Isaiah so horrified at his vision and why does he instruct the captains to "oil the shields?" What does verse 5 tell you about Israel's readiness?

8. What is God teaching Israel? What is He showing you in these passages? Can deliverance be found apart from God?

9. Read Isaiah 45:5-7, Amos 3:6-7, Jeremiah 29:11, and Romans 8:28. What do you learn about the Lord from these verses? How do these truths relate to your life and walk with God?

Prayer

Lord, whatever happens in my life, I know You determined it for my good and Your glory. You never let me be tempted by more than I can bear. Help me live in light of these truths when I'm tested. Strengthen my faith and give me grace to make it today. In Jesus' victorious name, Amen.

Depend On Him!

SYNOPSIS

Are you being tossed to and fro by empty doctrines and worldly philosophies? Do you depend on man's wisdom to find solutions to your problems? Today we'll explore the oracle to Israel – a nation that "did not depend on Him…."

 Where's That Verse?

CROSS-REFERENCES
Isaiah 14:24, 27; 36:12; 57:1
2 Chronicles 32:8
Psalms 119:38; 139:16
Ecclesiastes 3:7
Jeremiah 23:16
Joel 3:14
Matthew 7:6
Luke 15:4
John 18:9; 17:12
2 Corinthians 5:8

QUESTIONS

1. Observe Isaiah 21:1-17 and 22:1-13. Mark key words including *destruction* with red flames and time phrases with a green clock. Note in the margins what God addresses in each oracle and its location on your map. Also, review your observations of Isaiah 21:1-5 from the previous program.

2. What does the lookout report in the first oracle in chapter 21? Why is this sobering news to Israel?

3. How does Isaiah refer to his people in verse 10? Whose message is he delivering?

4. Summarize the main points of the oracle to Edom.

5. What do you learn about the people of Arabia? How quickly will their judgment take place?

6. Read the **Did You Know?** section and then answer the following questions about chapter 22:
   a. Where are the people in verse 1? Why?
   b. Note the verb tense in verse 2. How are they described?
   c. What happens to their people according to verses 2-3?
   d. Why does Isaiah weep? (v. 4) What's coming? (v. 5)
   e. What do you learn about the enemy in verses 6-7?
   f. How does Judah attempt to prepare for the siege? (vv. 8-11)
   g. In all their preparations, what do they fail to do?

7. Spend some time examining your life. Ask yourself who you depend on when things are good and bad. Then commit to live in total surrender to God's will.

8. Record a theme for Isaiah 21 in your **At A Glance** chart.

 **Did You Know?**

Sargon II wrote in 715 B.C. that he had defeated a number of Arabian tribes and deported them to Samaria.

If The Valley of Vision refers to the Kidron valley next to Jerusalem, the oracle is aimed at the southern kingdom of Judah.

Prayer
Lord, over and over this week You've confronted me with the truth that You control my life and do whatever it takes to bring my wandering heart back to You. Soften my heart O Lord… overpower me when I resist. Keep my eyes on Christ, the Author and Perfecter of faith. In His name, Amen.

Temporal or Eternal?

Isaiah 22:4-25; 23:1-18

Where's That Verse?

CROSS-REFERENCES

Isaiah 14:24, 28; 26:4; 37:12; 46:11

Genesis 21:33

2 Chronicles 32:7-9

Psalm 90:1-3; 93:2

Ezekiel 27:36

Joel 2

Romans 8:28

2 Corinthians 4:18; 5:1-3

James 4:6

Revelation 3:8

Did You Know?

Ancient Tyre and Sidon were situated in the area that is now Lebanon. At one time Beirut (Lebanon) was considered one of the most educated cities in the Middle East—a center for learning Middle Eastern culture. Civil war eventually destabilized and destroyed it.

SYNOPSIS

"Let us eat and drink, for tomorrow we may die" (Isaiah 22:13). Although this line was written thousands of years ago, the philosophy prevails today – men and women looking for instant gratification, fulfillment in things and people. Are your eyes focused on the temporal or the eternal?

QUESTIONS

1. Read Isaiah 22 and 23—the final oracles to the nations. Mark key words and time phrases as you have previously and ask the 5 W and H questions as you read.

2. Isaiah 22:12 begins with "therefore." Why does the Lord call His people to wail? Review the previous verses for context.

3. How do they behave instead? What does the Lord say then?

4. Verse 15 is addressed to an individual. Who is this person and why will the Lord judge him?

5. Who will replace this steward and what does God do for him?

6. What will happen *in that day* according to verse 25?

7. What do you learn about Tyre's reputation, livelihood, origin, benefactors, etc. from 23:1-8?

8. Why will the Lord judge Tyre? How?

9. Who is cited as an example of God's judgment? What happened to them? Who destroyed them?

10. What will happen 70 years after Tyre's judgment? Who will benefit from her prosperity this time?

11. Record themes for chapters 22 and 23 on your **At A Glance** chart.

12. As we conclude this week's theme on God's purpose and plans, what truths do you need to apply to your life? How is He speaking to your heart?

Prayer
Lord, even as I study Your fierce and righteous wrath, I'm reminded that You are good all the time and Your promises true. Stamp eternity on my heart so today's troubles don't overwhelm and blind me. I endure today for the hope of glory, so teach, correct, reprove, and train me in Your ways. Fill me with Your joy. In Jesus' name I pray, Amen.

A Day of Reckoning

SYNOPSIS

Today we'll move from God's judgments on nations In Isaiah's day to His final judgment on the world. Isaiah details the most horrific events yet in our study... a terrible reality to come. On that day, the world's trendsetters, powerful, and popular will face God's fierce wrath. No one will escape His hand.

QUESTIONS

1. Carefully read Isaiah 24:1-6. What will the Lord do to the earth and its people?

2. How are the people described in verse 2? What does this mean?

3. Read Romans 2:11 to understand God's view of man. Does worldly status benefit man in the day of judgment?

4. What do you learn about the earth from verses 3-4?

5. Who fades away? What does the repetition of this topic in Isaiah tell you about God?

6. What have people done to the earth according to verse 5?

7. What judgment do they face (v. 6)?

8. How will you respond to this knowledge? Are you of the world, denying a day of wrath and judgment, or of the faithful remnant, living in ways that please God?

Prayer
God, I believe this vast judgment will happen just as You have spoken. I want to fight the good fight and endure to the end. Lord, protect me from the traps of this world, its lures and seductions. Grant me boldness to speak the Word to this perishing world and in Your grace open ears and eyes to understand. In Jesus' name, Amen.

TODAY'S TEXT
Isaiah 24:1-6

Where's That Verse?

CROSS-REFERENCES
Isaiah 14:24; 5:20
Genesis 9:16
1 Corinthians 6:11
1 Thessalonians 4:1-6
2 Peter 3:3-4

Man's Corruption, the Earth's Pollution

TODAY'S TEXT
Isaiah 24:1-6

Where's That Verse?

CROSS-REFERENCES

Isaiah 24:21

Genesis 1:1-4, 22, 26-27; 2:8, 16-17; 3:1-6, 24; 4:8-16; 6:1-3, 5-8, 11-14, 18; 9:1, 5, 9, 12-14, 16-17; 15:17-18

Matthew 24:38

Romans 5:12

Philippians 2:15-16

2 Timothy 4:1-4

SYNOPSIS

Do you realize God created man for His pleasure? How did one man's rebellion set in motion a downward spiral leading to the most depraved and heinous sins? Today we'll revisit the coming judgment and examine what happened when man chose his way rather than God's.

QUESTIONS

1. Review Isaiah 24:1-6 and mark ⬛covenant⬛ in red with a yellow box. Also double underline *earth* in green (a geographical location) and shade it brown.

2. What three things are the inhabitants of the earth guilty of doing? Put a number by each in verse 5.

3. Let's establish some context to understand God's creation, His purpose for it, and how man violated God's "everlasting covenant." Read the following verses and note what you learn about God, man, and covenant.
   a. Creation – Genesis 1
   b. God's command to Adam – 2:16-17
   c. Adam and Eve's sin – 3:6
   d. Cain's sin – 4:9-16
   e. Noah and the Flood – 6:1-8, 11-18
   f. The Everlasting Covenant – 9:5-17

4. What did God create man to do?

5. Read Romans 5:12. How did Adam's sin impact future generations?

6. Why did God flood the world? What did you observe about man prior to the flood?

7. What does God require when man commits murder? Does society carry this out?

8. What happens to the earth when society doesn't execute justice? How does this help you understand why God will judge the earth?

9. In light of your study today, evaluate the command in 2 Timothy 4:1-4. What is your responsibility? Are you prepared to fulfill it? What is the urgency?

Prayer
Father I realized today that the day of the Lord is more than judgment on mankind, it's also vindication of innocent blood shed on earth. The headlines today are shocking – man's heart is corrupt and our society celebrates it. Come quickly Lord for the sake of the righteous who are persecuted for Your name. In Jesus' name, Amen.

"It Will Fall, Never To Rise Again"

SYNOPSIS

The world is partying, oblivious to a righteous and holy God in heaven. People who believe life ends at death do not believe sin will be punished. From this, necessarily, they have to believe all injustices win out. But God's Word says the day is coming when God will "render to every man according to what he has done" (Revelation 22:12).

QUESTIONS

1. Observe Isaiah 24 and continue marking *earth* and its pronouns. Also watch for time phrases like *in that day, then, after many days,* etc., which indicate event order.

2. Verse 6 says few men are left. How is life for them described in verses 7-13?

3. What does the analogy in verse 13 help you understand?

4. Who are "they" in verses 14-16a? What are they doing?

5. Why does Isaiah say "Woe is me" in verse 16b? What happens before God's judgment is complete?

6. What else do you learn about the survivors in verses 17-18? Can anyone escape?

7. Compare your observations of the earth in verses 19-20 with Revelation 16:18-19.

8. Who's punished in this day? What happens to them?

9. What happens at the end of these events? Compare this with Haggai 2:6-7 and Hebrews 12:25-29.

10. Finally, read 2 Peter 3:3-13 and note the repetition of *destruction* and *destroyed.*
    a. Who come in the last days? What are they saying?
    b. What will be destroyed and how?
    c. Why does the Lord wait?
    d. How should believers live in light of this destruction?
    e. What will the new heavens and earth be like?

11. What is your response to today's study? Awe? Fear? If the Lord comes in your lifetime, will you be among the faithful remnant crying out "Glory to the Righteous One"?

12. What has God given you from His Word to say to "scoffers" around you?

TODAY'S TEXT
Isaiah 24:1-21

 **Where's That Verse?**

CROSS-REFERENCES

Genesis 9:5-6

Haggai 2:3, 6-7

Romans 2:11

Philippians 2:15

Hebrews 12:25-29

2 Peter 3:3-4, 7, 9, 18

Revelation 6:10; 11:15-18; 16:18, 21

Prayer
Lord, we eagerly wait for the day when you will wipe away our tears and reward our faithfulness. But we're also thankful for your patience toward those who don't know you… my heart cries out for them. Lord, in Your mercy and for the glory of Your name send revival to the nations and churches so many more will enter Your kingdom. I pray in the name of Jesus, my Savior and Lord, Amen.

Judgment for the Host of Heaven

TODAY'S TEXT
Isaiah 24:21-23

Where's That Verse?

CROSS-REFERENCES

Genesis 6:1-2; 9:5

Deuteronomy 32:4

Job 1:6

Matthew 25:41

Mark 9:48

2 Corinthians 5:21

Ephesians 3:17; 6:12

2 Peter 2:2-4, 8-9

Jude 1:6

Revelation 12:7-12; 20:1-8, 10-15

SYNOPSIS

Although you may have *human* enemies, the Bible says ultimately your "struggle is not against flesh and blood, but against the rulers, against the powers, against the world forces of this darkness, against the spiritual forces of wickedness in the heavenly places" (Ephesians 6:12). You can be strong in the Lord when you rest in the truth that even Satan and his angels will face judgment.

QUESTIONS

1. Review Isaiah 24:21-23. Who will God punish? What will He do?

2. Look up "host of heaven" in Revelation 12:7-12.
   a. Who's at war?
   b. What's the immediate outcome?
   c. What happens afterward on earth?

3. Now read Revelation 20:1-7. Mark references to the *devil* with a red pitchfork and *thousand years* with a clock.
   a. What do you learn about Satan?
   b. Where does he spend a thousand years?
   c. Does this bear on the interpretation of Isaiah 24:21-23?

4. Observe 2 Peter 2:4, 9 (read 2:1-9 for context) and Jude 6. What is the purpose of the place described?

5. Read the account of the Great White Throne judgment in Revelation 20:10-15 and mark *lake of fire* with red flames.
   a. Who is thrown into the *lake of fire*?
   b. What happens there and for how long?
   c. What does Jesus say about hell in Mark 9:48 and Matthew 25:41?

6. Carefully read John 3:16-18 and 2 Corinthians 5:21. What is God's solution to man's dilemma?

Prayer

Father, You can rescue me from trials and temptations but You also have equipped me to stand firm in them with the sword of the Spirit. Help me walk above the world's sorrows and anxieties with joy and peace that evidences Your work in my life. Use my testimony to draw broken hearts to Your Son – the way, the truth, and the life – in whose name I pray, Amen.

Victory in Jesus!

PROGRAM 45

TODAY'S TEXT
Isaiah 24:21-23; 25:1-12

 Where's
That
Verse?

CROSS-REFERENCES

Isaiah 14:26; 24:1, 6

Mark 9:46

John 15:14, 18

Romans 6:23

1 Corinthians 15:42, 51-54,
56-58

2 Corinthians 4:4

Philippians 2:15

2 Peter 3:10

Revelation 20:15; 21:1-8,
22-23; 22:1-7, 12, 17

SYNOPSIS

Have you ever watched a marathon runner limp, even crawl across a finish line to receive some object of fleeting glory? Believers, too, are called to run a race, but it's to receive an imperishable prize. Jesus said He's coming soon and bringing eternal rewards with Him.

QUESTIONS

1. Read Isaiah 24:21-23 and 25:1-12. Mark time phrases and circle the phrase *He will swallow up death for all time.* Also double underline in green references to the mountain (Jerusalem) and shade them blue. Describe the subject shift from chapter 24 to 25.

2. What will follow God's judgment of "the host of heaven" and "the kings of the earth"?

3. Why does Isaiah praise God in 25:1-5? What do you learn about God's character from these verses? What does he compare God to?

4. What will God do for His people according to verses 6-8? How will they respond? Meditate on the majesty and wonder of this day.

5. Compare your observations in Isaiah with Revelation 21:1-8. What is repeated about death in the new heaven and earth?

6. What additional insight does 1 Corinthians 15:51-54, 56-58 give you? How are you supposed to live according to verse 58? Why?

7. Read Revelation 21:22-23 and 22:1-5 for a description of God's holy city. What else do you learn about His "bondservants"?

8. Now read Revelation 22:6-7, 12, and 17. Who is blessed? Describe God's invitation. Have you responded to it?

9. Look at the final verses in Isaiah 25. How does the fate of these people contrast with the destiny of God's people?

10. Record themes for chapters 24 and 25 on your **At A Glance** chart.

Prayer
Lord, we all stand on the threshold of eternity, waiting for the end of our short lives. For your children it's the beginning of all they've hoped and hungered for. I praise You, God Most High, for the plan You will complete in Your faithfulness to the righteous. Thank You for calling me to be Your child, an heir to the great inheritance in heaven. In Jesus' name, Amen.

Where's That Verse?

CROSS-REFERENCES
Isaiah 1:4, 7-9, 18; 2:2-4, 6-8; 5:1-2, 13-26; 6:1-3, 5, 7-9, 13; 7:2-4, 9, 14; 9:6; 11:1; 14:24; 19:23; 24:1, 5-6, 23; 26: 7, 19; 27:13

1 Timothy 6:15

Romans 7:18; 8:28

Peace in Turmoil

SYNOPSIS

How do you respond to God's promise of peace? Do you think your circumstances are too tough for it? Today we'll study this promise and how you can obtain it.

QUESTIONS

1. Review the previous chapters in this segment—Isaiah 24 and 25. What event is detailed? Why does it occur? What happens to the earth's inhabitants? To God's people?

2. Now read Isaiah 26:1-4, marking time phrases. What happens *in that day?*

3. Who will receive peace? How?

4. What is God called that tells us we can fully trust Him?

5. Think about the context of this segment in Isaiah. Why is Isaiah talking about peace and trust in God?

6. What circumstance dominates your life—an illness, relationship, child, job? How are you handling it?

7. Read Philippians 4:6-9. What does God command? What does He promise? What should we focus on – circumstances or God? How can you redirect your focus if you have let your situation overshadow the truth?

8. Finally, look up Romans 8:28. What hope does this verse give you? Ask God to help you experience His peace as He accomplishes His purposes in you.

Prayer
Father, I confess I have been shaken by stresses and let my emotions run wild. But Your Word says that while every *thing* changes, You, the everlasting Rock, never do. Lord, help me stand firm in this truth so I can testify to the world about the joy and peace You give Your children. I pray in the name of the very *Prince* of Peace, Amen!

The Heavenly City

SYNOPSIS

How does the world cope with pain? Tragedy? Injustice? What misguided movements, philosophies, and religions have resulted from man's attempt to deal with these things apart from the Most High God? When you put your trust in the Everlasting One, He preserves you with His peace even in the storms of life.

PROGRAM 47

TODAY'S TEXT
Isaiah 26:1-9

Where's
That
Verse?

CROSS-REFERENCES
Isaiah 1:2; 2:17; 11:16; 24:3-4; 25:9

Genesis 3:1, 5

Deuteronomy 31:30; 32:1-4

Hebrews 11:6, 13-14, 16

QUESTIONS

1. Observe Isaiah 26:1-9, marking *righteous(ness)* and *peace.* What do the righteous enter? How is "the righteous nation" described?

2. What do you learn about God from these verses? Compare this passage with Moses' song in Deuteronomy 32:1-4.

3. Now look up Hebrews 11:13-16 (read 1-12 for context). How are the people described in these verses? What has God prepared for them? How does this relate to Isaiah 26:1-2?

4. Contrast the "strong city" in Isaiah 26:1 with the "unassailable city" in verses 5-6. What will God do to this proud people?

5. What do you learn about the *righteous* in verse 7? How does God enable His people to stand firm and follow Him in adversity and difficult times?

6. While God pours out His judgment, what are His people doing?

7. What does God's judgment do according to verse 9?

8. Do you long for the things of God? For justice and righteousness? Are you set apart for Him, separated from the things of the world?

Prayer
Lord, Your Word commands us to live "sensibly, righteously and godly in this present age, looking for the blessed hope and appearing of . . . Jesus" (Titus 2:12-13). Our opposition is strong and its message loud. Make my path clear when difficulties come so I can live righteously. In Jesus' name, Amen.

Persevering Through Trials

SYNOPSIS

It's easy for life to knock us down, and when trials keep coming it's tempting to give up. Today we'll study God's sovereign purpose for these testings and how He leads the righteous through them. Press on . . . He's coming soon!

QUESTIONS

1. Observe Isaiah 26:7-16, then re-read verse 7. What does God do for the righteous?

2. Read Hebrews 10:32-39. What have the readers endured? How does the writer encourage them to press on? How should they live?

3. Compare your observations from Hebrews with Matthew 17:17-20. What enables believers to do the impossible?

4. How are the wicked and righteous contrasted in Isaiah 26:9-12? Consider who God softened and hardened by His judgments.

5. What did you learn about God's sovereignty from these verses in Isaiah?

6. Look at Jeremiah 14:1, 22; Amos 3:6, Job 36:30-32 and 37:10-12, and Psalm 148:8. What does God control? Are any circumstances in your life beyond His reach?

7. What do Psalm 119:67, 71 say about "affliction" and its purpose? Have trials brought you closer to God? Have they drawn you to study His Word?

8. What else do you learn about the righteous in Isaiah 26:12-13, 15-16? About the wicked in verse 14?

9. What truths from today's study can you apply to your life?

Prayer
Lord, Your Word reveals a vivid picture of the fate of the righteous and wicked. I see that only those who walk by faith endure. Father, grow my faith. I want to please You by doing the work You called me to. Strengthen me to persevere through trials and hardships. Use them to mold me into the image of Your Son, in whose name I pray, Amen.

Surpassing Peace for the Righteous

SYNOPSIS

Are you in such pain that you can hardly breathe? Is each moment agony? Well, God not only is with you, He also cares deeply for you! His Son intercedes for mercy and sustaining grace in your time of need.

QUESTIONS

1. Observe Isaiah 26:12-21, asking the 5W and Hs. Continue marking *earth, peace, God,* and the *righteous* including synonyms and pronouns.

2. What did you learn about God from these verses? What does He do for His people?

3. Study the description of God's people in verses 16-18. What are they *not* able to do?

4. Compare verse 14 with verse 19. Contrast the destinies of the two groups.

5. Now look up Daniel 12:2 and John 5:24-29. How do these verses relate?

6. What does God command His people in Isaiah 26:20? For how long?

7. What will the Lord do to the inhabitants of the earth according to verse 21? Relate this to Numbers 35:33.

8. What does He promise the righteous in Revelation 3:10?

9. Record a theme for Isaiah 26 on your **At A Glance** chart

TODAY'S TEXT
Isaiah 26:12-21

Where's
That
Verse?

CROSS-REFERENCES

Genesis 7:1, 16

Exodus 12

Numbers 35:33

Psalm 119:71

Daniel 12:2

Zechariah 4:6

John 1:1; 3:16; 5:24-30; 14:10

2 Corinthians 5:21

Revelation 3:10

Prayer
Lord You are my Shield and Great Reward. Although my heart aches today, I can sing Your praises because one day I will stand in Your presence and You will wipe away my tears. Sustain me in my grief and weakness. In Jesus' name, Amen.

PROGRAM 50

TODAY'S TEXT
Isaiah 27:1-13

Where's That Verse?

CROSS-REFERENCES

Isaiah 5:1-2; 11:11-12, 16; 24:1, 21; 26:1, 20-21

Genesis 3:5

Deuteronomy 4:27

2 Corinthians 5:8

Ephesians 2:2; 6:13, 17

1 Thessalonians 4:16-17

Revelation 12:9-12; 13:1, 3-4; 19:11-15, 19-20; 20:1-3, 7-10

The Serpent's Destiny

SYNOPSIS

We've studied two destinies for man—God's glorious city and the lake of fire. Now what about the evil one who rules wicked men and angels?

QUESTIONS

1. Review Isaiah 24:21, noting who God judges. Then read Isaiah 26:20-21 and 27:1 marking *in that day*. According to these verses, who does God punish?

2. How is Leviathan described? List your observations.

3. Now look up Genesis 3:1, 5, Revelation 12:9, and 13:1, 3-4. What do you learn about the serpent (dragon)? How is his power described? Who worships him?

4. Read Revelation 19:11-15, 19-20, and 20:1-3. What happens to the serpent and those who follow him? Who executes God's judgment? How?

5. Lastly, examine Revelation 20:7-10. What is the serpent's destiny?

6. How do all these verses compare with Isaiah 27:1?

7. Now read Isaiah 27:2-13, marking key words and time phrases. What do you learn about God in verses 1-6? About Israel?

8. How did God deal with Israel when they sinned against Him, according to verses 7-9?

9. What do you learn about "the fortified city" and its people? How does this contrast with the previous verses? (Recall references to "the unassailable city" in this segment of Isaiah.)

10. What does God promise at the end of this chapter? To whom?

11. Record a theme for chapter 27 on the **At A Glance** chart.

12. Think about the main points from this segment and meditate on how you can apply them to your life.

Prayer
Father, Your Word reveals Satan as the power working in evil men. His agenda is to kill, steal, and destroy Your marvelous creation. Lord, clothe me with Your full armor so I can stand firm against his schemes and equip me with the shield of faith that quenches his fiery attacks (Ephesians 6:11, 16). In Jesus' mighty name, Amen.

Understanding Your Enemies

SYNOPSIS

Do you know your enemies? Do you know your vulnerabilities – your personal weaknesses? Are your faith, home, and way of life threatened by a rising anti-Christian culture or religion? How can you stand firm in the Lord in the days ahead?

QUESTIONS

1. As we begin a new segment in Isaiah, read Isaiah 28–33 to get an overview. Mark the six *woes* and ask 5W and H questions as you observe them.

2. Locate the nations mentioned in these chapters on your map and note their proximities to Israel.

3. Briefly describe who and what the people of Israel relied on rather than God.

4. How does the spiritual condition of Israel at this time compare to your nation's? To yours?

5. What religious, political, and cultural enemies face your country?

6. What enemies are you dealing with personally—immorality, materialism, greed, legalism?

7. Look up 2 Peter 1:1-10. How has God equipped believers to stand? What are you responsible to do?

8. How does God want you to deal with your enemies? Ask Him for "a spirit of wisdom and of revelation in the knowledge of Him" (Ephesians 1:17) to live according to His ways in our corrupt and perverse world.

TODAY'S TEXT
Isaiah 31:1

Where's That Verse?

CROSS-REFERENCES

Isaiah 28:16; 64:8

Genesis 3:19

Jeremiah 13:11

Acts 20:27

Titus 1:1; 2:5

Did You Know?

Assyria was the predominant world empire from 900 to 686 B.C.

Prayer

Father, You told us to not fear those who can kill just the body, but to fear the One who can destroy both body and soul. Show me my weaknesses and help me fight them. As a believer in a hostile environment, make me strong in Your strength, ready to defend my beliefs and able to stand in them. In Jesus' name of victory I pray, Amen.

**Where's
That
Verse?**

CROSS-REFERENCES
**Isaiah 1:1; 5:13; 6:1; 7:1-4, 7, 9;
9:6; 14:24, 27-28; 24:1 26:3;
28:16; 29:1, 16; 30:15; 64:8**

Proverbs 29:25

John 6:37; 14:6

1 Peter 2:6

Getting the Big Picture

SYNOPSIS

Have you heard the threats of terrorism? Seen the chaos in nations around the world? Do these hate messages take hold of you, tear apart the quiet rest that belongs to you as one of the Lord's sheep? Take heart, believer! Look to Him who shepherds and preserves His people.

QUESTIONS

1. Today we will review the major segments of Isaiah covered so far in our study. Learning how each segment fits into the book helps us more accurately understand the book's overall theme.
   Begin by noting the following segment divisions on your **At A Glance** chart:
   a. Chapters 1-12
   b. Chapters 13-23
   c. Chapters 24-27
   d. Chapters 28-33

2. In the first segment, God primarily addresses Judah (Southern Kingdom) though He sometimes refers to Ephraim (Northern Kingdom).
   a. Review some of the key verses from this segment: Isaiah 1:2-4, 5:13, and 7:9.
   b. What have God's chosen people done to Him?
   c. What will happen to them?

3. The second segment contains oracles against surrounding nations.
   a. Review the nations God addresses and their relationships to Israel.
   b. Look up Isaiah 14:24, 27. What is God's message of hope amid these prophecies of destruction?

4. In the third segment, God addresses all inhabitants of the earth.
   a. Review Isaiah 24:1, 5, and 21 to learn what will happen.
   b. How does God assure the faithful remnant in 26:3?

5. The fourth segment is directed at Israel. Study key verse Isaiah 30:15 and commit it to memory. Meditate on its truth and think about how you can apply it to your daily walk.

6. Record a summary statement for each segment on your **At A Glance** chart.

Prayer
Lord, You've preserved Isaiah's message for thousands of years to teach Your people how to live in uncertain futures. Sustain me with these truths; write them on my heart so I will remember them when I'm tested. Grant me faith to trust You alone when I'm tempted to turn to man for salvation. In the name of Him who is the way, the truth, and the life, Amen.

Pride's Deadly Consequences

SYNOPSIS

Who's in control of your life? Think about it . . . what consumes most of your time and money? Are you serving God's interests primarily or your own? Israel grew complacent in their worship of God and succumbed to the pleasures of the world. The price was costly...

QUESTIONS

1. Observe Isaiah 28:1-13 with 5W and H questions. Mark *woe* with a red cloud shaded brown and *pride* with a red arrow pointing up (include synonyms). Also mark key words from your bookmark.

2. What did you learn from marking *woe?* Who is it addressed to and why?

3. Who will humble the proud kingdom and how? Describe His agent of judgment. What does the text say about when this will occur?

4. How does verse 1 contrast with verses 5-6?

5. What do you learn about "the priest and the prophet" in verses 7-8? What is God's point in verses 9-11, 13? What happens to them? Read the **Did You Know?** section for additional insight.

6. What have God's people rejected according to verse 12?

7. Compare your observations in Isaiah with Amos 6:1, 4-9. What else do you learn about Ephraim's pride and decadent lifestyle and God's judgment?

8. How can you apply these truths to your life? How does drunkenness and excessive living corrupt a man? Think of some modern examples whose lifestyles ruined them.

9. Read Ephesians 4:14. What are the consequences of following unsound, ungodly teachers? Who are you putting your trust in?

Prayer

John says if you love the world, the love of the Father is not in you (1 John 2:15). Lord, we live in an age of glossy magazines and flashy commercials that tell us we "deserve" it all. I confess at times I've bought into this sense of entitlement and overwhelming desire for things of the world. Cleanse my mind, Lord, and create in me a heart that wants what You want. In Jesus' name, Amen.

TODAY'S TEXT
Isaiah 28:1-13

Where's That Verse?

CROSS-REFERENCES

2 Chronicles 16:9

Amos 6:1, 4-9

John 8:32

Ephesians 1:14

2 Peter 1:3

Did You Know?

"The proud crown of the drunkards of Ephraim" (28:1, 3) is Samaria, the capital of the Northern Kingdom.

Assyria conquered Ephraim in 722 B.C.

The statements "Order on order, order on order, Line on line, line on line, A little here, a little there" (28:10, 13) include Hebrew monosyllables that sound like a child babbling—to mock the prophet's preaching.

Resisting Insults

**Where's
That
Verse?**

CROSS-REFERENCES
**Isaiah 1:1; 9:6; 11:1; 16:5;
24:1; 26:3**

Joshua 10:12

2 Samuel 5:20

Psalm 1:1-2

John 1:11-12; 14:6

Acts 20:27

1 Corinthians 15:58

1 Peter 2:4-7

2 Peter 3:3-6

SYNOPSIS

Peter says scoffers will come in the last days. Have you felt the sting of mocking? Are you standing against the assault of a popular secular culture that has rejected the Lord and His Word? Then embrace Peter's command "to grow in the grace and knowledge of our Lord and Savior Jesus Christ" (2 Peter 3:18). You'll find courage, strength, and wisdom to overcome opposition.

QUESTIONS

1. Re-read Isaiah 28:1-13 for context and then observe verses 14-29, marking key words. Who is the Lord talking to in these verses? What is their status in Jerusalem?

2. *Pride* is a key word in Isaiah. In what ways are these "scoffers" arrogant? What do they believe according to verse 15?

3. What will God do?

4. What is the "cornerstone" in verse 16? Look up 1 Peter 2:4-7.

5. What does God promise those who trust Him? What happens to those who don't?

6. Look up Joshua 10:12-14 and 2 Samuel 5:19-20 for background on Mount Perazim and the valley of Gibeon. What did the Lord do in these places?

7. What is His "unusual task" and "extraordinary work"? Relate it to verse 22 and Isaiah 24:1.

8. What does God tell this group to do in verses 23-29? What point does He illustrate in verse 29? How does this contrast with the group's mindset?

9. "The fear of the Lord is the beginning of wisdom" (Psalm 111:10). What wisdom can you glean from Psalm 1:1-2? Evaluate these verses in light of your study today.

10. Record a theme for Isaiah 28 on your **At A Glance** chart

Prayer
Father, foolish men and false teachers are drawing many to themselves, spreading the enticing message that man is invincible and controls his own fate. Please give me the true knowledge of Jesus Christ that counters every false way. Guard my mind and heart from messages that corrupt; strengthen me with Your wisdom from above. In Jesus' name, Amen.

The City of God

SYNOPSIS

What is wisdom, discernment, reverence for God? Does God require more than prayer and other rituals? Can you please Him simply by following rules? Today we'll examine God's holy city—the place He chose for His people to worship Him—to discover how we can live today in order to prepare for the future.

QUESTIONS

1. Read Isaiah 29, marking key words, time phrases, and geographical locations. Note especially the two woes and who they concern. Also watch for truths about God.

2. According to verses 1-4, what will God do to Ariel (Jerusalem)? Describe this judgment.

3. Read the **Did You Know?** section and record the dates of Jerusalem's captivity on your map.

4. Isaiah 29:5 begins with "but," introducing a contrast. Who is Israel delivered from and when? Who delivers the nation and how?

5. Why is the Lord going to judge Jerusalem?
   a. What do verses 1, 9-14 reveal about the people? Why are they ignorant of God's plans?
   b. What do verses 15-16 show about the hearts of the leaders?

6. Verses 17-24 call God's remnant to look ahead. What does He promise? How does He address rulers at this time? What will Jerusalem be like?

7. For historical context compare 2 Chronicles 36:14-20 with your observations of Isaiah 29. What else do you learn about the people of Jerusalem? About how God judged them?

8. Jesus prophesied the second destruction of Jerusalem in Luke 21:20-24. Carefully observe these verses.

9. Now read Matthew 24:15-30—a third destruction yet to occur. Does this passage relate to the redemption of Jerusalem in Isaiah 29? How is this redemption described and what enemies are destroyed? What additional insight do Zechariah 14:3 and 9 give?

10. What can you conclude about God's plan for Jerusalem? Think about the conflict around the city in the past and currently. Who's vying to possess it and will they succeed?

11. How can you apply today's program to your life? Describe your relationship with God—external ritual or heart commitment? Are you serving Him with body and soul?

12. Record a theme for Isaiah 29 on your **At A Glance** chart.

Prayer
Father I'm convicted of a flippant attitude toward You, taking for granted Your choosing and calling me to a life of holy service in the body of Christ. It's so much easier to "go through the motions" than to engage, receive, and obey Your instruction, reproof, and training in righteousness. Transform my mind through Your Word. Help me surrender my will to Yours. In Jesus' name, Amen.

TODAY'S TEXT
Isaiah 29:1-24

 Where's That Verse?

CROSS-REFERENCES
2 Chronicles 36:15-17, 20

Zechariah 14:2-3, 9

Malachi 4:2

Matthew 24:15-16, 21, 23, 27, 30

Luke 21:20-24

Philippians 2:10-11

 **Did You Know?**

Babylon destroyed Jerusalem in 586 B.C., about 100 years after Isaiah's prophesying ended. Jerusalem was destroyed again in A.D. 70 by the Romans.

Blessed Are Those Who Long For Him

TODAY'S TEXT
Isaiah 30:1-2, 18

Where's That Verse?

CROSS-REFERENCES
**Isaiah 1:2, 4, 18; 7:4, 7, 9;
20:1-4; 26:3; 30:1-2, 18; 31:1**

Psalm 119:104

Matthew 6:33

SYNOPSIS

Are you frantic for a plan to relieve your stress? Do you search self-help books and web sites for solutions? Do you turn to men for advice before God? Today we will study the third *woe* in this segment of Isaiah addressed to those who fail to wait on Him.

QUESTIONS

1. Observe Isaiah 30:1-2, 18, marking *woe* with a red cloud, shaded brown. Who is God talking to in these verses?

2. According to verse 1, what have they done?

3. Who do they trust for deliverance rather than God? (Cf. Isaiah 31:1.)

4. Review Isaiah 20, noting what you learn about Egypt.

5. How did King Ahaz exemplify the behavior of this rebellious people? What did God tell him in Isaiah 7:9? What path did he choose?

6. What do you learn about the Lord from Isaiah 30:18? Who is blessed?

7. Meditate on the truths from today's programs. Do you wait on the Lord, trusting His plans?

8. Is God's Word a roadmap for life concerning your home, relationships, finances, and everyday decisions? Who do you turn to in times of testing and trouble? Consider Psalm 119:104-105.

Prayer

Father, Your Word says those who walk by the Spirit won't carry out the desire of the flesh... and oh Lord, how my flesh wants to react! I want quick fixes to my problems and tangible results just like the rebellious people of Israel. Help me *patiently* follow the Spirit's gentle lead in all things at all times. *Your* blessing and peace can't be matched by *anything* in this world. In Jesus' name, Amen.

Beware False Teachers

SYNOPSIS

Do you really want to know God's will? His *whole* counsel, or just *some* of it…mixed in with advice that tickles ears and entices flesh? Religious programs and bookstores are crammed with messages of prosperity and healing—a thriving movement today. Your choices say a lot about where you are with God.

QUESTIONS

1. Read Isaiah 30:1-15 marking key words from your bookmark. What happens to "rebellious children" who ally with Egypt? Describe the alliance.

2. What are they doing with their wealth according to verse 6? Will their treacherous journey be worth it? Read 2 Kings 18:13-16 for additional context.

3. What does God command Isaiah to write? Why?

4. Compare verses 9-11 with Isaiah 1:4; 6:9-10 and Jeremiah 14:14. What do you learn about the faith of these people? What do they *want* to hear? Why?

5. Now look at Paul's warning to Timothy in 2 Timothy 4:1-4. What did he tell Timothy to do? Who can Timothy expect to oppose him?

6. Can you identify false teachers today? What's a typical message? What's its appeal?

7. How is Judah's fall described in Isaiah 30:12-14? Why is God judging them?

8. According to verse 15, what message did they reject?

9. Have you succumbed to teachers who tell you you're *entitled* to health and wealth and can actually *claim* them from God? Whose will do you want?

TODAY'S TEXT

Isaiah 30:1-15, 18

Where's That Verse?

CROSS-REFERENCES

Isaiah 6:9-13

Matthew 5:17-18

John 12:48

Philippians 1:29

2 Timothy 1:1; 3:1-5, 13-16; 4:1-3

Prayer

Lord, grant me discernment in these last days since many false teachers spread false messages for false personal gain. Help me differentiate truth and lie to test the spirits as the Apostle John commanded. In Your mercy, God, exalt the righteous and humiliate the wicked who lead others to destruction. In Jesus' precious name I pray, Amen.

Looking to the Arm of Flesh

Where's That Verse?

CROSS-REFERENCES

Isaiah 1:5-6, 18; 2:4; 32:1

Exodus 32:3-4, 9; 33:2-3, 12-15, 20-23; 34:5

Psalm 139:16

Proverbs 18:10-12

Jeremiah 29:11; 30:11

John 16:33

Romans 8:28

SYNOPSIS

How do you wait on the Lord in times of trouble and anxiety? What if you've blown it? Can you wait on someone you don't know or trust? When you know God as your strong tower and refuge, you can be confident He'll take care of you, even restore you to where He wants you to be.

QUESTIONS

1. Review Isaiah 30:1-15 for context, and then observe verses 15-26. Mark *therefore* with three red dots like a triangle and note the conclusions.

2. Who is Judah looking to for aid and protection against the Assyrians? What does God say about this country? What will happen?

3. What does He want His people to do according to verse 15? How do they respond?

4. How will they be humiliated by the enemy?

5. Verse 18 looks ahead. What do you learn about the Lord? What will He provide for His people?

6. Why does God tell His people what He will do in the future? Think about His judgments on their bad choices. Do they need a message of hope? Do they *deserve* one?

7. In verse 26 God says He will heal the bruise He inflicted. What can you conclude from this chapter about His purpose in bruising us? Are bruises a *final* product?

8. Consider your circumstances under the light of Romans 8:28 and Jeremiah 29:11. What hope do they give you? What does Jesus promise in John 16:33?

Prayer
Lord, I can think of so many foolish decisions and rash statements I've made because I didn't seek You first. I'm impulsive when I let anger, stress, and hurt control me. Help me Lord to wait on You, to wait for Your grace and compassion in my time of need. In Jesus' name, Amen.

God's Compassion for the Repentant

SYNOPSIS

Have you replaced your love for the Father with the love of money, possessions, people, school, work? Your flesh always wants to do this. Will you return to God? Can you?

QUESTIONS

1. Review Isaiah 30:18-26, then read verses 27-33 noting everything you learn about the Lord. Mark *hearing, listening* with a green ear and *anger* as you did previously.

2. What attributes of God do you see in this passage?

3. What will happen to Israel's enemies? How does God execute His judgment?

4. Now read Isaiah 31. How does this chapter parallel chapter 30? List similarities you observe about Egypt, God's restoration of Israel and His judgment on their enemies.

5. What does God call for in verse 6? How do John the Baptist and Jesus' messages in Matthew 3:1-3 and 4:17 compare? What's the common theme?

6. Isaiah 32:1-4 continues the thought of chapter 31. Read verses 1-4. What will this new kingdom be like? Compare this with Isaiah 6:8-10.

7. Record themes for Isaiah 30 and 31 on your **At A Glance** chart.

8. Have you, like Israel, "defected" from the Lord? What does God want you to do about it? Are *you* willing to do it?

9. What can you tell people who say "I can't be forgiven!" How does today's program help you understand the heart of God?

TODAY'S TEXT
Isaiah 30:27-33; 31:1-9; 32:1-4

Where's That Verse?

CROSS-REFERENCES
Isaiah 6:8-10; 30:1, 15, 18
Zechariah 14:2-4
Matthew 3:1-3; 4:17
John 4:23
Colossians 3:5
Hebrews 13:8
Revelation 19:15-16

Prayer
Father, thank you for Your compassion and saving grace in Your Son Jesus. When my heart goes astray, convict me but also lead me back—cause me to repent. I eagerly await Your kingdom where sin will no longer reign. In Jesus' holy and perfect name I pray, Amen.

Cast Off Complacency

TODAY'S TEXT
Isaiah 32:3, 5-20

Where's That Verse?

CROSS-REFERENCES

Isaiah 22:13; 30:13, 15, 18; 31:9; 40:3; 55:1

Judges 5:6-7

Psalms 25; 27:11-14; 62:1-2, 6-8

Ezekiel 36:27-29

Did You Know?

The prophecies in Isaiah 32 may have been given shortly before 701 B.C. when Assyrian King Sennacherib attacked several fortified cities in Judah.

SYNOPSIS

Did you know God once raised up a woman to save Israel? When the nation's faith diminished, morality disintegrated, and courage dried up, Judge Deborah followed God's call to lead her people to victory. Today, God is calling us to step out of complacency and step up as soldiers for Jesus Christ.

QUESTIONS

1. Observe Isaiah 32. Mark *hear (ear), righteousness,* and *wait* in distinctive ways with other key words, time phrases, and geographical locations. Watch for changes in verb tense and determine if texts are specifying near or far future events.

2. When do verses 1-8 occur? How is this time described?

3. What do you learn about the fool, rogue, and nobleman? Do these descriptions compare to anyone you know? What about you?

4. What does God say to the women in Israel? *When* is he speaking to them?

5. Consider the context of this segment. Why are the women "complacent"? Who do they think will save them?

6. Why does God tell them to mourn? For what? For how long?

7. What will it be like after the Spirit is poured out? When will this occur?

8. Are you ready to take action—to stand in the gap for this generation, society, country? Are you boldly speaking truth and interceding on their behalf? Does your lifestyle proclaim God's standards?

9. Spend your remaining study time meditating on Psalms 25 and 62:1, 2, 6-8. Mark every reference to *wait* and note what you learn.

Prayer
Lord, our culture exalts the wicked and demeans the righteous. I pray for Your mercy on this godless generation blind to the truth. I ask You to mobilize the Church to boldly stand against deceivers and proponents of evil. And I ask for the Spirit of revival to sweep over our nation. In Jesus' name, Amen.

The Lord is My Treasure

SYNOPSIS

How can you remain stable when the world is so unstable? Stories of mass murder, genocide, brutality, and abuse are broadcast across the globe as wickedness grows. How would you stand if terror came closer to home?

QUESTIONS

1. As we prepare to observe Isaiah 33-35 this week, begin by meditating on key verse Isaiah 33:6. What is God to those who know Him?

2. Now think about today's headlines. What do they say about terror, radical religious groups, brutal regimes? Have they personally impacted your life? Are you afraid or resting in God's promises?

3. Look up 2 Timothy 3:1-5. What will man's character be like in the last days? Does this accurately describe people today?

4. What do you learn about man's fallen condition from Romans 1:28-32? Who does God give over to do these things?

5. What does Jesus say about the proliferation of terror and wickedness before the end of the age in Matthew 24:6-12?

6. Go back to Isaiah 33 and observe verses 1-2, 17-19. What does God say about the treacherous?

7. What does the remnant pray in verse 2? How will they endure the treacherous? What insight does this give you about living today?

8. What happens to the treacherous when the King returns? Does this help you face today's violence better?

TODAY'S TEXT
Isaiah 33:1-2, 6, 17-19

Where's That Verse?

CROSS-REFERENCES
Genesis 9:6, 9
Psalm 111:10
Matthew 24:12
Luke 21:28
Romans 1:19-20, 28-32
Ephesians 2:2-3
2 Timothy 3:1-5

Prayer
Lord, I'm rich because You've given me precious promises in Your Word. I don't have to fear man or any future; I know my life is in Your hands. But as the world around me grows increasingly wicked, be gracious to me. Give me strength to endure to the end. In the name of the Coming King, Amen.

PROGRAM 62

TODAY'S TEXT
Isaiah 33:1-17

Where's That Verse?

CROSS-REFERENCES
Isaiah 6:3; 9:6-7; 22:13; 26:3; 34:8; 40:1

Deuteronomy 32:39

Jeremiah 1:12; 6:14

Philippians 1:28

Hebrews 12:29

Hope for the Hopeless

SYNOPSIS

Judah faced a grim situation as Assyrian armies slowly overtook cities around Jerusalem. With terror, threats, and broken peace promises on every side, people were left with just one hope for salvation: God's faithfulness to His Word and to the faithful remnant of His people – a truth we can cling to today in our own treacherous world.

QUESTIONS

1. Observe Isaiah 33:1-17. Mark the key word *woe*. What enemy was dealing treacherously with Israel? Do you think verse 1 is general or applies only to this specific history? Explain your answer.

2. Verse 2 begins the remnant's prayer. What do they ask for? What do they acknowledge about the Lord?

3. Compare their prayer to what Paul says in Philippians 1:28. How should we face our spiritual opponents?

4. Analyze the conditions in Israel according to Isaiah 33:7-9. How are the leaders reacting to the enemy? How does the enemy regard the people? What's happening in the land?

5. How does God respond to Judah?

6. What two groups are contrasted in verses 13-17? What happens to each? Which one is blessed?

7. Read Jeremiah 1:12 and Isaiah 26:3. How do these verses comfort us in times of uncertainty?

8. Is God your treasure? Do you trust Him in times of distress?

Prayer
Lord, I'm reminded that You told us to rejoice in all things. Teach me to do this, to be content, in all circumstances trusting Your provision of strength to endure. I know You won't let me tempted by more than I can bear. I praise Your name because You are faithful to keep Your Word concerning Your children. In Jesus' name, Amen.

The Judge, The Lawgiver, The King

SYNOPSIS

Will peace ever exist in the Middle East? Will violence and terror in this region one day culminate in the battle of Armageddon? When God finally unfolds His plans for Israel, He will usher in His eternal kingdom for all believers: "The Lord has a day of vengeance, a year of recompense for the cause of Zion" (Isaiah 34:8).

QUESTIONS

1. Observe Isaiah 33:17-24. Ask the 5Ws and H to learn about Jerusalem (Zion) and the Lord in this passage.

2. Who is "the King" in verse 17? Look at the following verses for expanded descriptions:
   a. Isaiah 9:6-7
   b. Isaiah 32:1
   c. Isaiah 33:22
   d. Isaiah 43:15

3. Will peace ever come to Israel? Will it be free from terror and threats? List details the text gives you about the nation's status once the King begins His reign.

4. What do the final verses tell you about the redemption of Israel's people?

5. Record a theme for Isaiah 33 on your **At A Glance** chart.

6. Now read Isaiah 34:1-8. What does God say to the nations?

7. What will this slaughter be like? Read Revelation 14:18-20.

8. Now go back to Isaiah 34:1-8 and list everything you learn about God's wrath on the nations. Who is He fighting for?

9. How will this apocalyptic battle impact the heavens?

10. Isaiah 34 clearly states that only the righteous will see the King. Who is *your* king? Who or what rules *your* life?

TODAY'S TEXT
Isaiah 33:17-24; 34:1-8

 Where's That Verse?

CROSS-REFERENCES
Isaiah 9:6-7; 32:1; 33:1, 6; 43:15

Genesis 12:1-3

1 Chronicles 21:22

Matthew 6:9-10

Acts 17:28

Revelation 2:21; 5:9; 14:18-20

 **Did You Know?**

Ancient Ammon, Moab, and Edom occupied regions that are much of present-day Jordan.

Prayer
Lord, Your children wait for the day when justice, equality, and fairness will rule everyone. Until then, You're my King. Show Your grace in my life to others to turn their hearts toward You. In Jesus' name, Amen.

Edom's Example

Where's That Verse?

CROSS-REFERENCES

Isaiah 5:13; 6:13; 24:1, 23; 33:6

Genesis 12:2-3; 25:19, 22-34

Leviticus 3:3-4

Psalm 119:104

Acts 20:27

Romans 1:20

2 Corinthians 5:21; 12:9

Hebrews 12:15-17

1 John 2:2

Did You Know?

Edom means "red."

SYNOPSIS

Will peace ever exist in the Middle East? Hebrews 12:15-16 says "See to it that no one comes short of the grace of God... that there be no immoral or godless person like Esau, who sold his own birthright for a single meal." Jacob's twin is the epitome of someone looking for the instant gratification that ignores painful consequences ahead. Today we'll examine this man's rash choice and its connection with our study of Isaiah.

QUESTIONS

1. Observe Isaiah 34:6-17. Mark **Edom** and its pronouns in red, then double underline it in green. Also mark geographical locations and time phrases such as *forever and ever.* Locate Edom on your map.

2. How is God's judgment on Edom described? For whose sake does He judge according to verse 8?

3. What happens to the land? How long will it remain in this condition?

4. Who will possess Edom? For how long?

5. Verse 16 says "For His mouth has commanded, and His Spirit has gathered them. . . ." What do you learn about God's sovereignty from this verse?

6. Look up the following verses for insight into Edom.
   a. Where did the name "Edom" come from?
   b. What do you learn about Esau?
   c. Who was his father? What covenant promise was fulfilled in his descendents?
   d. What did he sell? To whom?
   e. What's significant about this action? What were firstborns entitled to? What did Esau miss out on?
   f. Relate this to Hebrews 12:15-17. What truths can you apply to your life?

7. Isaiah 34:5 says the people of Edom were "devoted to destruction." Why is this nation an example to other nations? To you? How do you need to respond?

Prayer
Lord, like Esau, the world wants Your blessing without changing its ways. But I want to repent from disobedience and obey Your commands from my heart. You've provided salvation from my sins in Your Son Jesus; now help me conduct myself honorably and do the work of service. Amen.

Marked for Eternity

TODAY'S TEXT
Isaiah 35:1-10

SYNOPSIS

We studied Edom's origin, but why will God's wrath fall so heavily on this one nation? What marked Esau's descendents for destruction? Today we'll see how God's promise to Abraham ties into Edom's demise.

Where's That Verse?

CROSS-REFERENCES
Isaiah 33:6
Genesis 12:1-3; 25:7-34
Leviticus 11:44
Numbers 20:14-21
Jeremiah 49:7-22
Ezekiel 35:3-15
Obadiah 1
Romans 3:23
2 Corinthians 5:21
Hebrews 12:14-17
1 Peter 1:7, 16
1 John 2:2

QUESTIONS

1. Review Isaiah 34 and your notes about Edom. Who did the Edomites descend from? What is his connection to Israel?

2. What's going to happen to Edom?

3. Now look up Genesis 12:1-3. What does God promise Abraham? Who will He curse?

4. Read Numbers 20:14-21, marking references to *Edom* including pronouns.
   a. What does Israel request?
   b. How does Edom respond?

5. Look up Jeremiah 49:16-22, Obadiah 1, and Ezekiel 35:3-15, marking references to *Edom* including pronouns and synonyms like Mount Seir and Bozrah as before.
   a. How do these passages compare with Isaiah 34?
   b. Why will God judge Edom? Be specific, and list the verses that answer.
   c. How do these cross-references relate to God's promise to Abraham?
   d. What can you conclude generally about how God deals with nations that attack Israel today?

6. Now read Isaiah 35:1-10. Locate the Arabah region on your map and its proximity to Edom. Note how the land is described in verse 1. What is so amazing about blossoms and springs in this area?

7. Describe the promises in these verses? Who are they for?

8. What do you learn about "the Highway of Holiness"? Who will walk on it?

9. To summarize, contrast Edom's path with the path of the redeemed. What is the destiny of each? Which path are *you* on?

10. Record themes for Isaiah 34 and 35 on your **At A Glance** chart.

11. If you aren't walking in the ways of the Lord, study the following verses: 1 Peter 1:16, Hebrews 12:14, and Romans 3:23. What does God require and what is man's problem? Now look up 2 Corinthians 5:21 and 1 John 2:2. What is God's solution?

Prayer
Father, Paul says you "delivered us from the domain of darkness, and transferred us to the kingdom of Your beloved Son, in whom we have redemption, the forgiveness of sins" (Colossians 1:13-14). These promises of a kingdom with "everlasting joy," "gladness," and where "sorrow and sighing flee away" are for me. Thank You, thank You. I am simply in awe of Your holiness and righteousness. In Jesus' name, Amen.

PROGRAM 66

TODAY'S TEXT
Isaiah 36:1-5

Where's
That
Verse?

CROSS-REFERENCES
**Isaiah 1:1, 9; 6:1, 5, 7-9, 13;
9:6; 7:1-3, 5-9, 11-14; 24:1,
5; 33:1, 17; 35:8, 10**

2 Samuel 7:13-14

Romans 8:28

The Enemy's Challenge

SYNOPSIS

Today our study moves from prophetic to historic as the prophet describes the setting in Judah under King Hezekiah. Though documentary in nature, this segment is rich with application from one man's struggle to lead his people, serve the Lord, and withstand overwhelming fear as the world's greatest enemy threatens to overtake him.

QUESTIONS

1. Observe Isaiah 36:1-5, marking time phrases and geographical locations. When does this chapter begin? What is happening?

2. Who comes to Jerusalem? Where does he meet Hezekiah's men?

3. How does the enemy challenge Hezekiah? What does he ask him?

4. What was Ahaz's relationship to Hezekiah (1 Kings 16:20)? Now review Isaiah 7:1-13.

   a. What similar problem did he face? (Note how his situation parallels Hezekiah's.)

   b. What does God tell Ahaz about his enemies? What is key to his success, according to verse 9?

5. How did Ahaz and Hezekiah react to their respective enemies? Who did they turn to? Compare 2 Kings 16:5, 7 with 2 Kings 19:1.

6. Although we haven't looked at the outcome of Hezekiah's situation yet, what has your study on Isaiah revealed about how God uses adverse circumstances in the lives of His people? Review Romans 8:28.

7. What is the spiritual value of being tested by enemies? How have you benefited from this experience?

Prayer
Father, I have chosen two paths at different times in my life, but only one resulted in blessing—when I turned to You with my whole heart. God, You are so faithful; You work miracles in impossible situations. You are glorified when I trust You in the midst of a trial. Teach me more Lord as I continue to study. In Jesus' name, Amen.

The Enemy's Tactics

TODAY'S TEXT
Isaiah 36:2-11

SYNOPSIS

"**What is this confidence you have?**" (Isaiah 36:4) Do skeptics ask you this question? When you face troubles, are they hard on your heels, scrutinizing your every word, emotion, and choice? God can turn these trials and difficulties into blessings, faithful one. Stand firm and your confidence will result in great glory and reward!

Where's That Verse?

CROSS-REFERENCES

Isaiah 31:1

1 Kings 13:18

2 Kings 18:1-4

2 Chronicles 30:1-2

Proverbs 7:16-19, 27

Matthew 4:3-7

Acts 20:27-32

Galatians 1:10

QUESTIONS

1. Begin your study today by looking at Hezekiah's character. Study 2 Kings 18:1-7 and 2 Chronicles 29:1-5, 10 and 30:1 to observe his relationship with the Lord and how he led God's people. List what you learn about him.

2. Now read Isaiah 36:2-11, carefully observing Rabshakeh's questions and statements. How does he try to weaken the people's confidence in Hezekiah? In God?

3. Why do you think Rabshakeh mentions the tearing down of the high places and altars to idols? Consider who's listening to his words (v. 11).

4. What "bargain" does he propose? Why would this deal be a compromise with the enemy?

5. According to Rabshakeh who sent the Assyrians to capture Jerusalem? What's he trying to do with this tactic?

6. How do Hezekiah's officials respond in verse 11? What's their concern?

7. Think about Paul and Jesus. What did they say when they were given opportunities to compromise? Look up Galatians 1:10, Acts 20:27, and Matthew 4:3-10.

8. Are you being tested? Are you tempted to compromise your loyalty to God? Who are you trusting in?

9. Whose voice are you listening to? How did Satan and Rabshakeh distort God's Word? For what purpose? What do you need to know?

Did You Know?

The historical background of the reigns of kings from Uzziah through Hezekiah is found in 2 Kings 15–20 and 2 Chronicles 26–32. We suggest you read this to get a thorough perspective of the times.

Prayer

Father, the enemy's agenda is to kill, steal, and destroy the faith and loyalty of Your children. Equip me with the Word to fight off his attacks. Help me follow the examples of Jesus and Paul who trusted You when they were tested and continued to proclaim Your name. I want a testimony that glorifies You and blesses others. In Jesus' name, Amen.

Resisting Compromise

Where's That Verse?

CROSS-REFERENCES

Deuteronomy 33:27

Job 13:15

Psalms 56:3; 103:19

Proverbs 21:1; 29:25

Daniel 3:17-18

Joel 1:8, 13

Malachi 2:16

1 Corinthians 10:13; 12:26

2 Timothy 1:7

Hebrews 13:4

Did You Know?

The Ivvahian people worshipped the gods Hamath and Arpad referred to in verse 19. The Assyrians conquered them and took them to Israel to replace the people they took into exile. Since their gods didn't come to their rescue, Sennacherib used them as an example to try to scare Jerusalem into surrendering in 701 B.C.

SYNOPSIS

When doubt has crept in and fear has settled in your heart, and the enemy's presence feels overpowering, you have two choices: fully walk in the power and knowledge God has given you or compromise with the enemy. Today, we'll discuss how to identify the enemy's methods and counterattack with God's Word.

QUESTIONS

1. Review Isaiah 36:1-10, then read Isaiah 36:11-22 and 37:1-10. Continue to analyze the enemy's statements. Think about why he says what he does.

2. Why do Hezekiah's men ask Rabshakeh to speak Aramaic? What does Rabshakeh say? What is he trying to do?

3. What does Rabshakeh say about Hezekiah? What incentive does he offer them to betray their king?

4. How does the enemy try to marginalize the Lord? Who does he compare Him to? Read the **Did You Know?** section for additional insight. Read 2 Chronicles 32:1-19 for additional context.

5. How do Hezekiah and his men respond to the enemy's blasphemy?

6. What do they ask Isaiah? How does Isaiah answer?

7. How does God intervene? What does this teach you about God's character? Look up Psalm 103:19.

8. Record a theme for Isaiah 36 on your **At A Glance** chart.

9. How can you get rid of fear? Read 2 Timothy 1:7 and Psalm 56:3.

10. When you're tempted to give up, how can 1 Corinthians 10:13 strengthen you?

11. Memorize the following verses: Deuteronomy 33:27, Proverbs 29:25, and Job 13:15. Ask God to write them on your heart—arsenal verses to cling to when the enemy attacks.

Prayer

Oh Lord, help me to never doubt You. Strengthen my heart to trust You completely when the enemy attacks. I don't want to be unfaithful when challenged and rendered useless for the kingdom. Use the verses I've studied today to equip me as a soldier for Christ, prepared in the day of battle. In Jesus' name, Amen.

A Living Epistle to the World

TODAY'S TEXT
Isaiah 37:14-38; 38:1-6

Where's
That
Verse?

CROSS-REFERENCES
Deuteronomy 32:39
2 Samuel 7:12-13
Psalm 31:15; 56:8; 139:2-3, 16
Jeremiah 13:11; 32:27
Zechariah 2:8
Romans 8:28-29
2 Corinthians 5:8
2 Timothy 4:10, 17
1 Peter 1:7
Revelation 2:9-11

SYNOPSIS

Do you know your life is a living epistle to those who don't know the Lord? When you confidently face hardships and illnesses, God uses your trust to testify to the world. You reveal Christ as you submit to God's will.

QUESTIONS

1. Observe Isaiah 37:8-38, watching the order of events. Mark *remnant* and *pride* as you did before and also time phrases.

2. What is Rabshakeh's final message to Hezekiah? What does Hezekiah do with it?

3. Analyze Hezekiah's prayer in verses 14-20. What attributes of God does he believe in? Why does he ask for deliverance?

4. Why is God willing to respond favorably to Hezekiah's requests? List the verses that give you the answers.

5. What does God say about Assyria?

6. What sign does God give Hezekiah?

7. God says "I will defend this city to save it for My own sake and for my servant David's sake" (Isaiah 37:35). How does this relate to 2 Samuel 7:12-13?

8. How does God miraculously fight for His people? How did Sennacherib's life end? Compare this with 2 Chronicles 32:20-23.

9. Record a theme for Isaiah 37 on your **At A Glance** chart.

10. Now read Isaiah 38:1-6—an event that occurred before Assyria attacked Jerusalem. What's wrong with Hezekiah? How does he respond to the news?

11. What does Isaiah say to him?

12. Reflect on how the following cross-references can strengthen your faith when you face death: Psalms 31:15 and 139:16, Revelation 2:9-11, 2 Corinthians 5:8.

13. What have you learned about God today that you can apply to your life? How will these truths encourage you to remain faithful in your current situation, hardship, or illness? How can you encourage others?

Prayer
Father, Hezekiah faced insurmountable circumstances, but in the end Your name was glorified and he was exalted in the land. Paul says it's our privilege to share in Christ's sufferings and Lord, and when our minds are set on eternity we can embrace this perspective. Whatever happens to me, help me maintain this attitude of trust and thanksgiving for Your sovereign plan. In Jesus' mighty name I pray, Amen.

Hezekiah's Blessing

Where's That Verse?

CROSS-REFERENCES

Numbers 6:24-25

2 Chronicles 32:24-26, 30-31

Romans 8:28

1 Corinthians 15:54

2 Corinthians 5:1, 8

Philippians 1:23; 3:10

Did You Know?

Merodach-Baladan (Isaiah 39:1) ruled from 721-710 B.C. and again from 703-702 B.C. His rule preceded Sennacherib's invasion of Judah in 701.

SYNOPSIS

Illness is a reality in this fallen world—a painful one that sometimes bereaves people of their loved ones. But it can also be a blessing—something God uses to draw us closer to Him. Today we'll conclude our glimpse into King Hezekiah's reign and how he dealt with his failing health.

QUESTIONS

1. Read Isaiah 38. What does verse 6 tell you about when these events occurred?

2. Now read 2 Kings 20 and 2 Chronicles 32:24-31. What additional details do you learn from these cross-references?

3. How did God respond to Hezekiah's prayer? What sign did He give?

4. Carefully re-read Hezekiah's record of his illness and recovery, and then answer the following questions.
   a. How did he feel about dying?
   b. What did he believe about God?
   c. What new perspective on life did he gain?
   d. How did his illness draw him closer to God?

5. Read Isaiah 39. Why did the Babylonian king visit Hezekiah? What did Hezekiah show him?

6. How did Hezekiah acquire so much wealth? In light of Assyria's campaign through the region, why do you think Babylon was interested to learn about Israel's assets?

7. What does Isaiah say to him after this meeting?

8. Think about Hezekiah's thoughts in verse 8 and what you saw in 2 Chronicles 32:24. Was he right? What event followed his recovery?

9. Record themes for Isaiah 38 and 39 on your **At A Glance** chart.

10. Spend the remainder of your study time reflecting on the truths you've learned from this first major division of Isaiah. What have you learned about sin and repentance, pride and humility, defeat and redemption, God's wrath and compassion?

Prayer
Heavenly Father, thank You for preserving Isaiah for us . . . it contains so many essential precepts for life. Reveal more and more of its truths to me as I meditate on all I've studied. And Lord, keep me humble. I don't want to become proud from this knowledge; I want to use it for Your service, glorifying and honoring You in everything. In Jesus' name, Amen.

Isaiah At A Glance

Book Theme:

Author:

Purpose:

Historical Setting:

Key Words:

SEGMENT DIVISIONS		CHAPTER THEMES
		1
		2
		3
		4
		5
		6
		7
		8
		9
		10
		11
		12
		13
		14
		15
		16
		17
		18
		19
		20
		21
		22
		23
		24
		25
		26
		27
		28
		29
		30
		31
		32
		33
		34
		35
		36
		37
		38
		39

Solomon's Temple

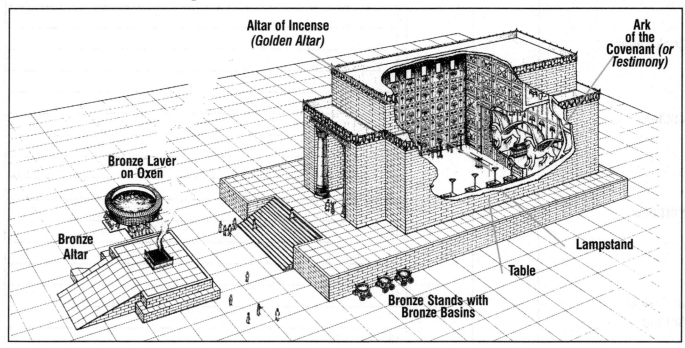

Altar of Incense
(Golden Altar)

Ark
of the
Covenant (or
Testimony)

Bronze Laver
on Oxen

Bronze
Altar

Lampstand

Table

Bronze Stands with
Bronze Basins

Temple Furnishings

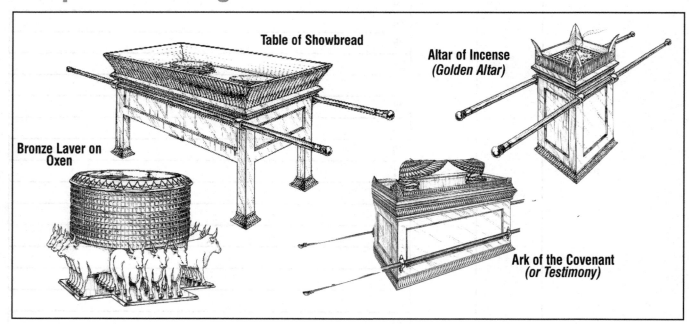

Table of Showbread

Altar of Incense
(Golden Altar)

Bronze Laver on
Oxen

Ark of the Covenant
(or Testimony)

Maps

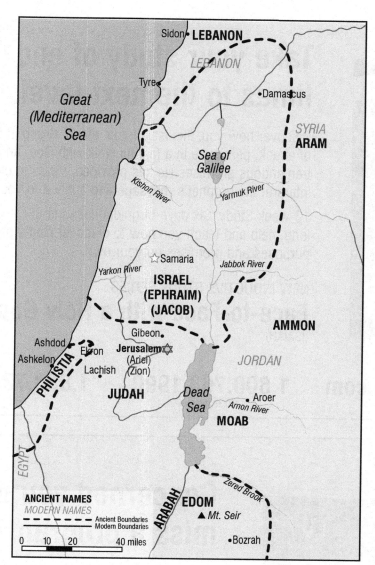

Great (Mediterranean) Sea

Sidon • **LEBANON**

LEBANON

Tyre •

• Damascus

SYRIA

ARAM

Sea of Galilee

Kishon River

Yarmuk River

☆ Samaria

Yarkon River

ISRAEL (EPHRAIM) (JACOB)

Jabbok River

Gibeon •

AMMON

Ashdod •

Ekron •

Jerusalem ☆ (Ariel) (Zion)

Ashkelon •

PHILISTIA

Lachish •

JUDAH

JORDAN

Dead Sea

• Aroer

Arnon River

MOAB

EGYPT

Zered Brook

ARABAH

EDOM

▲ Mt. Seir

• Bozrah

ANCIENT NAMES
MODERN NAMES
— — — Ancient Boundaries
———— Modern Boundaries

0 10 20 40 miles

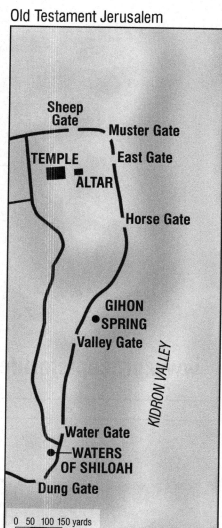

Old Testament Jerusalem

Sheep Gate

Muster Gate

TEMPLE

East Gate

ALTAR

Horse Gate

GIHON SPRING

Valley Gate

KIDRON VALLEY

Water Gate

WATERS OF SHILOAH

Dung Gate

0 50 100 150 yards

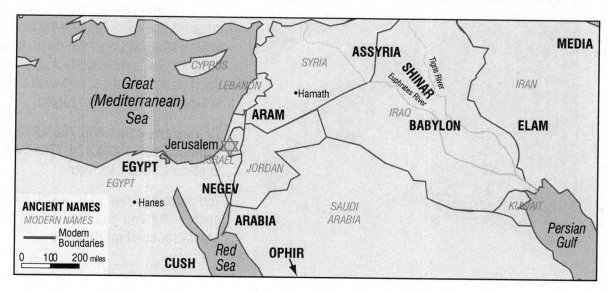

Great (Mediterranean) Sea

CYPRUS

ASSYRIA

MEDIA

SYRIA

Tigris River

SHINAR

IRAN

LEBANON

ARAM

• Hamath

Euphrates River

Jerusalem ☆

ISRAEL

BABYLON

IRAQ

ELAM

EGYPT

EGYPT

JORDAN

NEGEV

ARABIA

SAUDI ARABIA

KUWAIT

ANCIENT NAMES
MODERN NAMES
———— Modern Boundaries

0 100 200 miles

• Hanes

Persian Gulf

CUSH

Red Sea

OPHIR

Take your study of end times to the next level.

Discover how you, like Isaiah, can stand strong in the face of attack, persevere in a faithful walk with God, and claim the tremendous promises He has provided. Learn to observe and interpret the prophet's message and apply it to your life.

13-week Study. Six days of guided lessons, 20 to 30 minutes long, help and teach you how to discover God's precepts, purposes and promises on your own.

NEW INDUCTIVE STUDY SERIES
Face-to-Face with a Holy God
(ISAIAH)

www.preceptsforlife.com
ONLINE

1.800.763.1990
TELEVISION

1.888.734.7707
RADIO

Concerned you might miss a program?

Don't be! You can get a CD or DVD of this program and mark the Observation Worksheets as you study at your own pace. It will be like going to God's Bible school and having the Holy Spirit as your professor. He will take the things of God and reveal them to you.

TV viewers, call 1.800.763.1990, radio listeners, call 1.888.734.7707! We'll be happy to place an order for you!

You can also listen to or watch the programs online whenever you want on our website **www.PreceptsForLife.com.**

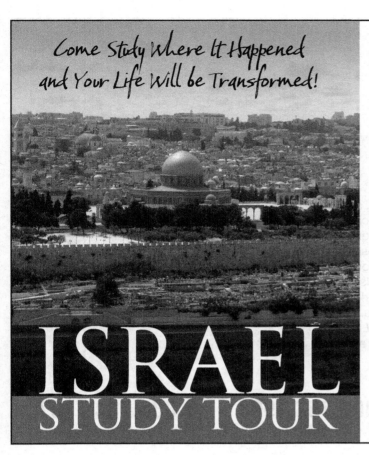
75

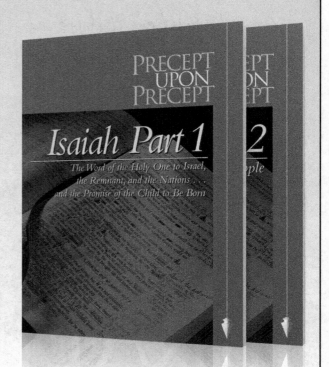
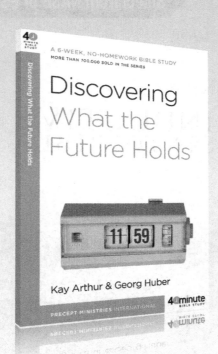

ISAIAH 1
Observation Worksheet

Chapter Theme _____

THE vision of Isaiah the son of Amoz concerning Judah and Jerusalem, which he saw during the reigns of Uzziah, Jotham, Ahaz *and* Hezekiah, kings of Judah.

2   Listen, O heavens, and hear, O earth;
    For the L ORD speaks,
     "Sons I have reared and brought up,
     But they have revolted against Me.

3   "An ox knows its owner,
    And a donkey its master's manger,
    But Israel does not know,
    My people do not understand."

4   Alas, sinful nation,
    People weighed down with iniquity,
    Offspring of evildoers,
    Sons who act corruptly!
    They have abandoned the L ORD,
    They have despised the Holy One of Israel,
    They have turned away from Him.

5   Where will you be stricken again,
    As you continue in *your* rebellion?
    The whole head is sick
    And the whole heart is faint.

6   From the sole of the foot even to the head
    There is nothing sound in it,
    Only bruises, welts and raw wounds,
    Not pressed out or bandaged,
    Nor softened with oil.

7   Your land is desolate,
    Your cities are burned with fire,
    Your fields—strangers are devouring them in your presence;

It is desolation, as overthrown by strangers.

8   The daughter of Zion is left like a shelter in a vineyard,

Like a watchman's hut in a cucumber field, like a besieged city.

9   Unless the LORD of hosts

Had left us a few survivors,

We would be like Sodom,

We would be like Gomorrah.

10   Hear the word of the LORD,

You rulers of Sodom;

Give ear to the instruction of our God,

You people of Gomorrah.

11   "What are your multiplied sacrifices to Me?"

Says the LORD.

"I have had enough of burnt offerings of rams

And the fat of fed cattle;

And I take no pleasure in the blood of bulls, lambs or goats.

12   "When you come to appear before Me,

Who requires of you this trampling of My courts?

13   "Bring your worthless offerings no longer,

Incense is an abomination to Me.

New moon and sabbath, the calling of assemblies—

I cannot endure iniquity and the solemn assembly.

14   "I hate your new moon *festivals* and your appointed feasts,

They have become a burden to Me;

I am weary of bearing *them.*

15   "So when you spread out your hands *in prayer,*

I will hide My eyes from you;

Yes, even though you multiply prayers,

I will not listen.

Your hands are covered with blood.

16   "Wash yourselves, make yourselves clean;

Remove the evil of your deeds from My sight.

Cease to do evil,

17   Learn to do good;

Seek justice,

Reprove the ruthless,
Defend the orphan,
Plead for the widow.

18 "Come now, and let us reason together,"
Says the LORD,
"Though your sins are as scarlet,
They will be as white as snow;
Though they are red like crimson,
They will be like wool.

19 "If you consent and obey,
You will eat the best of the land;

20 "But if you refuse and rebel,
You will be devoured by the sword."
Truly, the mouth of the LORD has spoken.

21 How the faithful city has become a harlot,
She *who* was full of justice!
Righteousness once lodged in her,
But now murderers.

22 Your silver has become dross,
Your drink diluted with water.

23 Your rulers are rebels
And companions of thieves;
Everyone loves a bribe
And chases after rewards.
They do not defend the orphan,
Nor does the widow's plea come before them.

24 Therefore the Lord GOD of hosts,
The Mighty One of Israel, declares,
"Ah, I will be relieved of My adversaries
And avenge Myself on My foes.

25 "I will also turn My hand against you,
And will smelt away your dross as with lye
And will remove all your alloy.

26   "Then I will restore your judges as at the first,
     And your counselors as at the beginning;
     After that you will be called the city of righteousness,
     A faithful city."

27   Zion will be redeemed with justice
     And her repentant ones with righteousness.

28   But transgressors and sinners will be crushed together,
     And those who forsake the LORD will come to an end.

29   Surely you will be ashamed of the oaks which you have desired,
     And you will be embarrassed at the gardens which you have chosen.

30   For you will be like an oak whose leaf fades away
     Or as a garden that has no water.

31   The strong man will become tinder,
     His work also a spark.
     Thus they shall both burn together
     And there will be none to quench *them*.

ISAIAH 2
Observation Worksheet

Chapter Theme _____

THE word which Isaiah the son of Amoz saw concerning Judah and Jerusalem.

2   Now it will come about that
     In the last days
     The mountain of the house of the Lord
     Will be established as the chief of the mountains,
     And will be raised above the hills;
     And all the nations will stream to it.

3   And many peoples will come and say,
     "Come, let us go up to the mountain of the Lord,
     To the house of the God of Jacob;
     That He may teach us concerning His ways
     And that we may walk in His paths."
     For the law will go forth from Zion
     And the word of the Lord from Jerusalem.

4   And He will judge between the nations,
     And will render decisions for many peoples;
     And they will hammer their swords into plowshares and their spears into pruning
          hooks.
     Nation will not lift up sword against nation,
     And never again will they learn war.

5   Come, house of Jacob, and let us walk in the light of the Lord.

6   For You have abandoned Your people, the house of Jacob,
     Because they are filled *with influences* from the east,
     And *they are* soothsayers like the Philistines,
     And they strike *bargains* with the children of foreigners.

7   Their land has also been filled with silver and gold
     And there is no end to their treasures;
     Their land has also been filled with horses
     And there is no end to their chariots.

8   Their land has also been filled with idols;
     They worship the work of their hands,

That which their fingers have made.

9   So the *common* man has been humbled
     And the man *of importance* has been abased,
     But do not forgive them.

10   Enter the rock and hide in the dust
     From the terror of the LORD and from the splendor of His majesty.

11   The proud look of man will be abased
     And the loftiness of man will be humbled,
     And the LORD alone will be exalted in that day.

12 For the LORD of hosts will have a day *of reckoning*
     Against everyone who is proud and lofty
     And against everyone who is lifted up,
     That he may be abased.

13   And *it will be* against all the cedars of Lebanon that are lofty and lifted up,
     Against all the oaks of Bashan,

14   Against all the lofty mountains,
     Against all the hills that are lifted up,

15   Against every high tower,
     Against every fortified wall,

16   Against all the ships of Tarshish
     And against all the beautiful craft.

17   The pride of man will be humbled
     And the loftiness of men will be abased;
     And the LORD alone will be exalted in that day,

18   But the idols will completely vanish.

19   *Men* will go into caves of the rocks
     And into holes of the ground
     Before the terror of the LORD
     And the splendor of His majesty,
     When He arises to make the earth tremble.

20   In that day men will cast away to the moles and the bats
     Their idols of silver and their idols of gold,
     Which they made for themselves to worship,

21   In order to go into the caverns of the rocks and the clefts of the cliffs
     Before the terror of the LORD and the splendor of His majesty,
     When He arises to make the earth tremble.

22   Stop regarding man, whose breath *of life* is in his nostrils;
     For why should he be esteemed?

ISAIAH 3
Observation Worksheet

Chapter Theme _____

FOR behold, the Lord GOD of hosts is going to remove from Jerusalem and Judah
Both supply and support, the whole supply of bread
And the whole supply of water;

2   The mighty man and the warrior,
The judge and the prophet,
The diviner and the elder,

3   The captain of fifty and the honorable man,
The counselor and the expert artisan,
And the skillful enchanter.

4   And I will make mere lads their princes,
And capricious children will rule over them,

5   And the people will be oppressed,
Each one by another, and each one by his neighbor;
The youth will storm against the elder
And the inferior against the honorable.

6   When a man lays hold of his brother in his father's house, *saying*,
"You have a cloak, you shall be our ruler,
And these ruins will be under your charge,"

7   He will protest on that day, saying,
"I will not be *your* healer,
For in my house there is neither bread nor cloak;
You should not appoint me ruler of the people."

8   For Jerusalem has stumbled and Judah has fallen,
Because their speech and their actions are against the LORD,
To rebel against His glorious presence.

9   The expression of their faces bears witness against them,
And they display their sin like Sodom;
They do not *even* conceal *it*.
Woe to them!
For they have brought evil on themselves.

10   Say to the righteous that *it will go* well *with them*,
For they will eat the fruit of their actions.

11   Woe to the wicked! *It will go* badly *with him,*
      For what he deserves will be done to him.

12   O My people! Their oppressors are children,
      And women rule over them.
      O My people! Those who guide you lead *you* astray
      And confuse the direction of your paths.

13   The LORD arises to contend,
      And stands to judge the people.

14   The LORD enters into judgment with the elders and princes of His people,
      "It is you who have devoured the vineyard;
      The plunder of the poor is in your houses.

15   "What do you mean by crushing My people
      And grinding the face of the poor?"
      Declares the Lord GOD of hosts.

16   Moreover, the LORD said, "Because the daughters of Zion are proud
      And walk with heads held high and seductive eyes,
      And go along with mincing steps
      And tinkle the bangles on their feet,

17   Therefore the Lord will afflict the scalp of the daughters of Zion with scabs,
      And the LORD will make their foreheads bare."

18   In that day the Lord will take away the beauty of *their* anklets, headbands, crescent ornaments,

19   dangling earrings, bracelets, veils,

20   headdresses, ankle chains, sashes, perfume boxes, amulets,

21   finger rings, nose rings,

22   festal robes, outer tunics, cloaks, money purses,

23   hand mirrors, undergarments, turbans and veils.

24   Now it will come about that instead of sweet perfume there will be putrefaction;
      Instead of a belt, a rope;
      Instead of well-set hair, a plucked-out scalp;
      Instead of fine clothes, a donning of sackcloth;
      And branding instead of beauty.

25   Your men will fall by the sword
      And your mighty ones in battle.

26   And her gates will lament and mourn,
      And deserted she will sit on the ground.

ISAIAH 4
Observation Worksheet

Chapter Theme _____

FOR seven women will take hold of one man in that day, saying, "We will eat our own bread and wear our own clothes, only let us be called by your name; take away our reproach!"

2   In that day the Branch of the LORD will be beautiful and glorious, and the fruit of the earth *will be* the pride and the adornment of the survivors of Israel.

3   It will come about that he who is left in Zion and remains in Jerusalem will be called holy—everyone who is recorded for life in Jerusalem.

4   When the Lord has washed away the filth of the daughters of Zion and purged the bloodshed of Jerusalem from her midst, by the spirit of judgment and the spirit of burning,

5   then the LORD will create over the whole area of Mount Zion and over her assemblies a cloud by day, even smoke, and the brightness of a flaming fire by night; for over all the glory will be a canopy.

6   There will be a shelter to *give* shade from the heat by day, and refuge and protection from the storm and the rain.

ISAIAH 5
Observation Worksheet

Chapter Theme _____

LET me sing now for my well-beloved

    A song of my beloved concerning His vineyard.

    My well-beloved had a vineyard on a fertile hill.

2   He dug it all around, removed its stones,

    And planted it with the choicest vine.

    And He built a tower in the middle of it

    And also hewed out a wine vat in it;

    Then He expected *it* to produce *good* grapes,

    But it produced *only* worthless ones.

3   "And now, O inhabitants of Jerusalem and men of Judah,

    Judge between Me and My vineyard.

4   "What more was there to do for My vineyard that I have not done in it?

    Why, when I expected *it* to produce *good* grapes did it produce worthless ones?

5   "So now let Me tell you what I am going to do to My vineyard:

    I will remove its hedge and it will be consumed;

    I will break down its wall and it will become trampled ground.

6   "I will lay it waste;

    It will not be pruned or hoed,

    But briars and thorns will come up.

    I will also charge the clouds to rain no rain on it."

7   For the vineyard of the LORD of hosts is the house of Israel

    And the men of Judah His delightful plant.

    Thus He looked for justice, but behold, bloodshed;

    For righteousness, but behold, a cry of distress.

8   Woe to those who add house to house *and* join field to field,

    Until there is no more room,

    So that you have to live alone in the midst of the land!

9   In my ears the LORD of hosts *has sworn,* "Surely, many houses shall become desolate,
     Even great and fine ones, without occupants.

10   "For ten acres of vineyard will yield *only* one bath *of wine,*
     And a homer of seed will yield *but* an ephah of grain."

11   Woe to those who rise early in the morning that they may pursue strong drink,
     Who stay up late in the evening that wine may inflame them!

12   Their banquets are *accompanied* by lyre and harp, by tambourine and flute, and by
         wine;
     But they do not pay attention to the deeds of the LORD,
     Nor do they consider the work of His hands.

13   Therefore My people go into exile for their lack of knowledge;
     And their honorable men are famished,
     And their multitude is parched with thirst.

14   Therefore Sheol has enlarged its throat and opened its mouth without measure;
     And Jerusalem's splendor, her multitude, her din *of revelry* and the jubilant within her,
         descend *into it.*

15   So the *common* man will be humbled and the man of *importance* abased,
     The eyes of the proud also will be abased.

16   But the LORD of hosts will be exalted in judgment,
     And the holy God will show Himself holy in righteousness.

17   Then the lambs will graze as in their pasture,
     And strangers will eat in the waste places of the wealthy.

18   Woe to those who drag iniquity with the cords of falsehood,
     And sin as if with cart ropes;

19   Who say, "Let Him make speed, let Him hasten His work, that we may see *it;*
     And let the purpose of the Holy One of Israel draw near
     And come to pass, that we may know *it!*"

20   Woe to those who call evil good, and good evil;
     Who substitute darkness for light and light for darkness;
     Who substitute bitter for sweet and sweet for bitter!

21   Woe to those who are wise in their own eyes
     And clever in their own sight!

22   Woe to those who are heroes in drinking wine
     And valiant men in mixing strong drink,

23   Who justify the wicked for a bribe,

And take away the rights of the ones who are in the right!

24 Therefore, as a tongue of fire consumes stubble
And dry grass collapses into the flame,
So their root will become like rot and their blossom blow away as dust;
For they have rejected the law of the LORD of hosts
And despised the word of the Holy One of Israel.

25 On this account the anger of the LORD has burned against His people,
And He has stretched out His hand against them and struck them down.
And the mountains quaked, and their corpses lay like refuse in the middle of the
   streets.
For all this His anger is not spent,
But His hand is still stretched out.

26 He will also lift up a standard to the distant nation,
And will whistle for it from the ends of the earth;
And behold, it will come with speed swiftly.

27 No one in it is weary or stumbles,
None slumbers or sleeps;
Nor is the belt at its waist undone,
Nor its sandal strap broken.

28 Its arrows are sharp and all its bows are bent;
The hoofs of its horses seem like flint and its *chariot* wheels like a whirlwind.

29 Its roaring is like a lioness, and it roars like young lions;
It growls as it seizes the prey
And carries *it* off with no one to deliver *it*.

30 And it will growl over it in that day like the roaring of the sea.
If one looks to the land, behold, there is darkness *and* distress;
Even the light is darkened by its clouds.

ISAIAH 6
Observation Worksheet

Chapter Theme _____

IN the year of King Uzziah's death I saw the Lord sitting on a throne, lofty and exalted, with the train of His robe filling the temple.

2   Seraphim stood above Him, each having six wings: with two he covered his face, and with two he covered his feet, and with two he flew.

3   And one called out to another and said,

"Holy, Holy, Holy, is the LORD of hosts,

The whole earth is full of His glory."

4   And the foundations of the thresholds trembled at the voice of him who called out, while the temple was filling with smoke.

5   Then I said,

"Woe is me, for I am ruined!

Because I am a man of unclean lips,

And I live among a people of unclean lips;

For my eyes have seen the King, the LORD of hosts."

6   Then one of the seraphim flew to me with a burning coal in his hand, which he had taken from the altar with tongs.

7   He touched my mouth *with it* and said, "Behold, this has touched your lips; and your iniquity is taken away and your sin is forgiven."

8   Then I heard the voice of the Lord, saying, "Whom shall I send, and who will go for Us?" Then I said, "Here am I. Send me!"

9   He said, "Go, and tell this people:

'Keep on listening, but do not perceive;

Keep on looking, but do not understand.'

10   "Render the hearts of this people insensitive,

Their ears dull,

And their eyes dim,

Otherwise they might see with their eyes,

Hear with their ears,

Understand with their hearts,

And return and be healed."

11   Then I said, "Lord, how long?" And He answered,
       "Until cities are devastated *and* without inhabitant,
        Houses are without people
        And the land is utterly desolate,

12   "The LORD has removed men far away,
        And the forsaken places are many in the midst of the land.

13   "Yet there will be a tenth portion in it,
        And it will again be *subject* to burning,
        Like a terebinth or an oak
        Whose stump remains when it is felled.
        The holy seed is its stump."

Chapter Theme _____

NOW it came about in the days of Ahaz, the son of Jotham, the son of Uzziah, king of Judah, that Rezin the king of Aram and Pekah the son of Remaliah, king of Israel, went up to Jerusalem to *wage* war against it, but could not conquer it.

2 When it was reported to the house of David, saying, "The Arameans have camped in Ephraim," his heart and the hearts of his people shook as the trees of the forest shake with the wind.

3 Then the Lord said to Isaiah, "Go out now to meet Ahaz, you and your son Shear-jashub, at the end of the conduit of the upper pool, on the highway to the fuller's field,

4 and say to him, 'Take care and be calm, have no fear and do not be fainthearted because of these two stubs of smoldering firebrands, on account of the fierce anger of Rezin and Aram and the son of Remaliah.

5 'Because Aram, *with* Ephraim and the son of Remaliah, has planned evil against you, saying,

6 "Let us go up against Judah and terrorize it, and make for ourselves a breach in its walls and set up the son of Tabeel as king in the midst of it,"

7 thus says the Lord God: "It shall not stand nor shall it come to pass.

8 "For the head of Aram is Damascus and the head of Damascus is Rezin (now within another 65 years Ephraim will be shattered, *so that it is* no longer a people),

9 and the head of Ephraim is Samaria and the head of Samaria is the son of Remaliah. If you will not believe, you surely shall not last." ' "

10 Then the Lord spoke again to Ahaz, saying,

11 "Ask a sign for yourself from the Lord your God; make *it* deep as Sheol or high as heaven."

12 But Ahaz said, "I will not ask, nor will I test the Lord!"

13 Then he said, "Listen now, O house of David! Is it too slight a thing for you to try the patience of men, that you will try the patience of my God as well?

14 "Therefore the Lord Himself will give you a sign: Behold, a virgin will be with child and bear a son, and she will call His name Immanuel.

15 "He will eat curds and honey at the time He knows *enough* to refuse evil and choose good.

16 "For before the boy will know *enough* to refuse evil and choose good, the land whose two kings you dread will be forsaken.

17 "The Lord will bring on you, on your people, and on your father's house such days as have never come since the day that Ephraim separated from Judah, the king of Assyria."

18 In that day the Lord will whistle for the fly that is in the remotest part of the rivers of Egypt and for the bee that is in the land of Assyria.

19 They will all come and settle on the steep ravines, on the ledges of the cliffs, on all the thorn bushes and on all the watering places.

20 In that day the Lord will shave with a razor, hired from regions beyond the Euphrates (*that is*, with the king of Assyria), the head and the hair of the legs; and it will also remove the beard.

21 Now in that day a man may keep alive a heifer and a pair of sheep;

22 and because of the abundance of the milk produced he will eat curds, for everyone that is left within the land will eat curds and honey.

23 And it will come about in that day, that every place where there used to be a thousand vines, *valued* at a thousand *shekels* of silver, will become briars and thorns.

24 *People* will come there with bows and arrows because all the land will be briars and thorns.

25 As for all the hills which used to be cultivated with the hoe, you will not go there for fear of briars and thorns; but they will become a place for pasturing oxen and for sheep to trample.

ISAIAH 8
Observation Worksheet

Chapter Theme _____

THEN the Lᴏʀᴅ said to me, "Take for yourself a large tablet and write on it in ordinary letters: Swift is the booty, speedy is the prey.

2 "And I will take to Myself faithful witnesses for testimony, Uriah the priest and Zechariah the son of Jeberechiah."

3 So I approached the prophetess, and she conceived and gave birth to a son. Then the Lᴏʀᴅ said to me, "Name him Maher-shalal-hash-baz;

4 for before the boy knows how to cry out 'My father' or 'My mother,' the wealth of Damascus and the spoil of Samaria will be carried away before the king of Assyria."

5 Again the Lᴏʀᴅ spoke to me further, saying,

6 "Inasmuch as these people have rejected the gently flowing waters of Shiloah
   And rejoice in Rezin and the son of Remaliah;

7 "Now therefore, behold, the Lord is about to bring on them the strong and abundant waters of the Euphrates,
   Even the king of Assyria and all his glory;
   And it will rise up over all its channels and go over all its banks.

8 "Then it will sweep on into Judah, it will overflow and pass through,
   It will reach even to the neck;
   And the spread of its wings will fill the breadth of your land, O Immanuel.

9 "Be broken, O peoples, and be shattered;
   And give ear, all remote places of the earth.
   Gird yourselves, yet be shattered;
   Gird yourselves, yet be shattered.

10 "Devise a plan, but it will be thwarted;
   State a proposal, but it will not stand,
   For God is with us."

11 For thus the Lᴏʀᴅ spoke to me with mighty power and instructed me not to walk in the way of this people, saying,

12 "You are not to say, '*It is* a conspiracy!'
   In regard to all that this people call a conspiracy,
   And you are not to fear what they fear or be in dread of *it*.

13 "It is the Lᴏʀᴅ of hosts whom you should regard as holy.

And He shall be your fear,

And He shall be your dread.

14 "Then He shall become a sanctuary;

But to both the houses of Israel, a stone to strike and a rock to stumble over,

And a snare and a trap for the inhabitants of Jerusalem.

15 "Many will stumble over them,

Then they will fall and be broken;

They will even be snared and caught."

16 Bind up the testimony, seal the law among my disciples.

17 And I will wait for the LORD who is hiding His face from the house of Jacob; I will even look eagerly for Him.

18 Behold, I and the children whom the LORD has given me are for signs and wonders in Israel from the LORD of hosts, who dwells on Mount Zion.

19 When they say to you, "Consult the mediums and the spiritists who whisper and mutter," should not a people consult their God? *Should they consult* the dead on behalf of the living?

20 To the law and to the testimony! If they do not speak according to this word, it is because they have no dawn.

21 They will pass through the land hard-pressed and famished, and it will turn out that when they are hungry, they will be enraged and curse their king and their God as they face upward.

22 Then they will look to the earth, and behold, distress and darkness, the gloom of anguish; and *they will be* driven away into darkness.

ISAIAH 9
Observation Worksheet

Chapter Theme _____

BUT there will be no *more* gloom for her who was in anguish; in earlier times He treated the land of Zebulun and the land of Naphtali with contempt, but later on He shall make *it* glorious, by the way of the sea, on the other side of Jordan, Galilee of the Gentiles.

2   The people who walk in darkness
     Will see a great light;
     Those who live in a dark land,
     The light will shine on them.

3   You shall multiply the nation,
     You shall increase their gladness;
     They will be glad in Your presence
     As with the gladness of harvest,
     As men rejoice when they divide the spoil.

4   For You shall break the yoke of their burden and the staff on their shoulders,
     The rod of their oppressor, as at the battle of Midian.

5   For every boot of the booted warrior in the *battle* tumult,
     And cloak rolled in blood, will be for burning, fuel for the fire.

6   For a child will be born to us, a son will be given to us;
     And the government will rest on His shoulders;
     And His name will be called Wonderful Counselor, Mighty God,
     Eternal Father, Prince of Peace.

7   There will be no end to the increase of *His* government or of peace,
     On the throne of David and over his kingdom,
     To establish it and to uphold it with justice and righteousness
     From then on and forevermore.
     The zeal of the LORD of hosts will accomplish this.

8   The Lord sends a message against Jacob,
     And it falls on Israel.

9   And all the people know *it*,
     That is, Ephraim and the inhabitants of Samaria,
     Asserting in pride and in arrogance of heart:

10   "The bricks have fallen down,

But we will rebuild with smooth stones;
The sycamores have been cut down,
But we will replace *them* with cedars."

11 Therefore the LORD raises against them adversaries from Rezin
And spurs their enemies on,

12 The Arameans on the east and the Philistines on the west;
And they devour Israel with gaping jaws.
In *spite of* all this, His anger does not turn away
And His hand is still stretched out.

13 Yet the people do not turn back to Him who struck them,
Nor do they seek the LORD of hosts.

14 So the LORD cuts off head and tail from Israel,
Both palm branch and bulrush in a single day.

15 The head is the elder and honorable man,
And the prophet who teaches falsehood is the tail.

16 For those who guide this people are leading *them* astray;
And those who are guided by them are brought to confusion.

17 Therefore the Lord does not take pleasure in their young men,
Nor does He have pity on their orphans or their widows;
For every one of them is godless and an evildoer,
And every mouth is speaking foolishness.
In *spite of* all this, His anger does not turn away
And His hand is still stretched out.

18 For wickedness burns like a fire;
It consumes briars and thorns;
It even sets the thickets of the forest aflame
And they roll upward in a column of smoke.

19 By the fury of the LORD of hosts the land is burned up,
And the people are like fuel for the fire;
No man spares his brother.

20 They slice off *what is* on the right hand but *still* are hungry,
And they eat *what is* on the left hand but they are not satisfied;
Each of them eats the flesh of his own arm.

21 Manasseh *devours* Ephraim, and Ephraim Manasseh,
And together they are against Judah.
In *spite of* all this, His anger does not turn away
And His hand is still stretched out.

Chapter Theme _____

WOE to those who enact evil statutes
        And to those who constantly record unjust decisions,
2   So as to deprive the needy of justice
        And rob the poor of My people of *their* rights,
        So that widows may be their spoil
        And that they may plunder the orphans.
3   Now what will you do in the day of punishment,
        And in the devastation which will come from afar?
        To whom will you flee for help?
        And where will you leave your wealth?
4   Nothing *remains* but to crouch among the captives
        Or fall among the slain.
        In *spite of* all this, His anger does not turn away
        And His hand is still stretched out.

5   Woe to Assyria, the rod of My anger
        And the staff in whose hands is My indignation,
6   I send it against a godless nation
        And commission it against the people of My fury
        To capture booty and to seize plunder,
        And to trample them down like mud in the streets.
7   Yet it does not so intend,
        Nor does it plan so in its heart,
        But rather it is its purpose to destroy
        And to cut off many nations.
8   For it says, "Are not my princes all kings?
9   "Is not Calno like Carchemish,
        Or Hamath like Arpad,
        Or Samaria like Damascus?
10   "As my hand has reached to the kingdoms of the idols,
        Whose graven images *were* greater than those of Jerusalem and Samaria,

11   Shall I not do to Jerusalem and her images

        Just as I have done to Samaria and her idols?"

12   So it will be that when the Lord has completed all His work on Mount Zion and on

        Jerusalem, *He will say,* "I will punish the fruit of the arrogant heart of the king of Assyria

        and the pomp of his haughtiness."

13   For he has said,

        "By the power of my hand and by my wisdom I did *this,*

        For I have understanding;

        And I removed the boundaries of the peoples

        And plundered their treasures,

        And like a mighty man I brought down *their* inhabitants,

14   And my hand reached to the riches of the peoples like a nest,

        And as one gathers abandoned eggs, I gathered all the earth;

        And there was not one that flapped its wing or opened *its* beak or chirped."

15   Is the axe to boast itself over the one who chops with it?

        Is the saw to exalt itself over the one who wields it?

        That would be like a club wielding those who lift it,

        Or like a rod lifting *him who* is not wood.

16   Therefore the Lord, the GOD of hosts, will send a wasting disease among his stout

                warriors;

        And under his glory a fire will be kindled like a burning flame.

17   And the light of Israel will become a fire and his Holy One a flame,

        And it will burn and devour his thorns and his briars in a single day.

18   And He will destroy the glory of his forest and of his fruitful garden, both soul and

                body,

        And it will be as when a sick man wastes away.

19   And the rest of the trees of his forest will be so small in number

        That a child could write them down.

20   Now in that day the remnant of Israel, and those of the house of Jacob who have escaped,

        will never again rely on the one who struck them, but will truly rely on the LORD, the

        Holy One of Israel.

21   A remnant will return, the remnant of Jacob, to the mighty God.

22   For though your people, O Israel, may be like the sand of the sea,

        Only a remnant within them will return;

        A destruction is determined, overflowing with righteousness.

23 For a complete destruction, one that is decreed, the Lord GOD of hosts will execute in the midst of the whole land.

24 Therefore thus says the Lord GOD of hosts, "O My people who dwell in Zion, do not fear the Assyrian who strikes you with the rod and lifts up his staff against you, the way Egypt *did.*

25 "For in a very little while My indignation *against you* will be spent and My anger *will be directed* to their destruction."

26 The LORD of hosts will arouse a scourge against him like the slaughter of Midian at the rock of Oreb; and His staff will be over the sea and He will lift it up the way *He did* in Egypt.

27 So it will be in that day, that his burden will be removed from your shoulders and his yoke from your neck, and the yoke will be broken because of fatness.

28 He has come against Aiath,

He has passed through Migron;

At Michmash he deposited his baggage.

29 They have gone through the pass, *saying,*

"Geba will be our lodging place."

Ramah is terrified, and Gibeah of Saul has fled away.

30 Cry aloud with your voice, O daughter of Gallim!

Pay attention, Laishah *and* wretched Anathoth!

31 Madmenah has fled.

The inhabitants of Gebim have sought refuge.

32 Yet today he will halt at Nob;

He shakes his fist at the mountain of the daughter of Zion, the hill of Jerusalem.

33 Behold, the Lord, the GOD of hosts, will lop off the boughs with a terrible crash;

Those also who are tall in stature will be cut down

And those who are lofty will be abased.

34 He will cut down the thickets of the forest with an iron *axe,*

And Lebanon will fall by the Mighty One.

ISAIAH 11
Observation Worksheet

Chapter Theme _____

THEN a shoot will spring from the stem of Jesse,

      And a branch from his roots will bear fruit.

2   The Spirit of the LORD will rest on Him,

      The spirit of wisdom and understanding,

      The spirit of counsel and strength,

      The spirit of knowledge and the fear of the LORD.

3   And He will delight in the fear of the LORD,

      And He will not judge by what His eyes see,

      Nor make a decision by what His ears hear;

4   But with righteousness He will judge the poor,

      And decide with fairness for the afflicted of the earth;

      And He will strike the earth with the rod of His mouth,

      And with the breath of His lips He will slay the wicked.

5   Also righteousness will be the belt about His loins,

      And faithfulness the belt about His waist.

6   And the wolf will dwell with the lamb,

      And the leopard will lie down with the young goat,

      And the calf and the young lion and the fatling together;

      And a little boy will lead them.

7   Also the cow and the bear will graze,

      Their young will lie down together,

      And the lion will eat straw like the ox.

8   The nursing child will play by the hole of the cobra,

      And the weaned child will put his hand on the viper's den.

9   They will not hurt or destroy in all My holy mountain,

      For the earth will be full of the knowledge of the LORD

      As the waters cover the sea.

10   Then in that day

      The nations will resort to the root of Jesse,

Who will stand as a signal for the peoples;
And His resting place will be glorious.

11   Then it will happen on that day that the Lord
Will again recover the second time with His hand
The remnant of His people, who will remain,
From Assyria, Egypt, Pathros, Cush, Elam, Shinar, Hamath,
And from the islands of the sea.

12   And He will lift up a standard for the nations
And assemble the banished ones of Israel,
And will gather the dispersed of Judah
From the four corners of the earth.

13   Then the jealousy of Ephraim will depart,
And those who harass Judah will be cut off;
Ephraim will not be jealous of Judah,
And Judah will not harass Ephraim.

14   They will swoop down on the slopes of the Philistines on the west;
Together they will plunder the sons of the east;
They will possess Edom and Moab,
And the sons of Ammon will be subject to them.

15   And the LORD will utterly destroy
The tongue of the Sea of Egypt;
And He will wave His hand over the River
With His scorching wind;
And He will strike it into seven streams
And make *men* walk over dry-shod.

16   And there will be a highway from Assyria
For the remnant of His people who will be left,
Just as there was for Israel
In the day that they came up out of the land of Egypt.

ISAIAH 12
Observation Worksheet

Chapter Theme _____

THEN you will say on that day,

"I will give thanks to You, O LORD;

For although You were angry with me,

Your anger is turned away,

And You comfort me.

2 "Behold, God is my salvation,

I will trust and not be afraid;

For the LORD GOD is my strength and song,

And He has become my salvation."

3 Therefore you will joyously draw water

From the springs of salvation.

4 And in that day you will say,

"Give thanks to the LORD, call on His name.

Make known His deeds among the peoples;

Make *them* remember that His name is exalted."

5 Praise the LORD in song, for He has done excellent things;

Let this be known throughout the earth.

6 Cry aloud and shout for joy, O inhabitant of Zion,

For great in your midst is the Holy One of Israel.

ISAIAH 13
Observation Worksheet

Chapter Theme _____

THE oracle concerning Babylon which Isaiah the son of Amoz saw.

2   Lift up a standard on the bare hill,
     Raise your voice to them,
     Wave the hand that they may enter the doors of the nobles.

3   I have commanded My consecrated ones,
     I have even called My mighty warriors,
     My proudly exulting ones,
     To *execute* My anger.

4   A sound of tumult on the mountains,
     Like that of many people!
     A sound of the uproar of kingdoms,
     Of nations gathered together!
     The Lord of hosts is mustering the army for battle.

5   They are coming from a far country,
     From the farthest horizons,
     The Lord and His instruments of indignation,
     To destroy the whole land.

6   Wail, for the day of the Lord is near!
     It will come as destruction from the Almighty.

7   Therefore all hands will fall limp,
     And every man's heart will melt.

8   They will be terrified,
     Pains and anguish will take hold of *them;*
     They will writhe like a woman in labor,
     They will look at one another in astonishment,
     Their faces aflame.

9   Behold, the day of the Lord is coming,
     Cruel, with fury and burning anger,
     To make the land a desolation;
     And He will exterminate its sinners from it.

10   For the stars of heaven and their constellations
Will not flash forth their light;
The sun will be dark when it rises
And the moon will not shed its light.

11   Thus I will punish the world for its evil
And the wicked for their iniquity;
I will also put an end to the arrogance of the proud
And abase the haughtiness of the ruthless.

12   I will make mortal man scarcer than pure gold
And mankind than the gold of Ophir.

13   Therefore I will make the heavens tremble,
And the earth will be shaken from its place
At the fury of the LORD of hosts
In the day of His burning anger.

14   And it will be that like a hunted gazelle,
Or like sheep with none to gather *them,*
They will each turn to his own people,
And each one flee to his own land.

15   Anyone who is found will be thrust through,
And anyone who is captured will fall by the sword.

16   Their little ones also will be dashed to pieces
Before their eyes;
Their houses will be plundered
And their wives ravished.

17   Behold, I am going to stir up the Medes against them,
Who will not value silver or take pleasure in gold.

18   And *their* bows will mow down the young men,
They will not even have compassion on the fruit of the womb,
Nor will their eye pity children.

19   And Babylon, the beauty of kingdoms, the glory of the Chaldeans' pride,
Will be as when God overthrew Sodom and Gomorrah.

20   It will never be inhabited or lived in from generation to generation;
Nor will the Arab pitch *his* tent there,
Nor will shepherds make *their flocks* lie down there.

21   But desert creatures will lie down there,
      And their houses will be full of owls;
      Ostriches also will live there, and shaggy goats will frolic there.

22   Hyenas will howl in their fortified towers
      And jackals in their luxurious palaces.
      Her *fateful* time also will soon come
      And her days will not be prolonged.

ISAIAH 14
Observation Worksheet

Chapter Theme _____

WHEN the Lord will have compassion on Jacob and again choose Israel, and settle them in their own land, then strangers will join them and attach themselves to the house of Jacob.

2 The peoples will take them along and bring them to their place, and the house of Israel will possess them as an inheritance in the land of the Lord as male servants and female servants; and they will take their captors captive and will rule over their oppressors.

3 And it will be in the day when the Lord gives you rest from your pain and turmoil and harsh service in which you have been enslaved,

4 that you will take up this taunt against the king of Babylon, and say,
    "How the oppressor has ceased,
      And how fury has ceased!

5 "The Lord has broken the staff of the wicked,
      The scepter of rulers

6 Which used to strike the peoples in fury with unceasing strokes,
      Which subdued the nations in anger with unrestrained persecution.

7 "The whole earth is at rest *and* is quiet;
      They break forth into shouts of joy.

8 "Even the cypress trees rejoice over you, *and* the cedars of Lebanon, *saying,*
      'Since you were laid low, no *tree* cutter comes up against us.'

9 "Sheol from beneath is excited over you to meet you when you come;
      It arouses for you the spirits of the dead, all the leaders of the earth;
      It raises all the kings of the nations from their thrones.

10 "They will all respond and say to you,
      'Even you have been made weak as we,
      You have become like us.

11 'Your pomp *and* the music of your harps
      Have been brought down to Sheol;
      Maggots are spread out *as your bed* beneath you
      And worms are your covering.'

12   "How you have fallen from heaven,
            O star of the morning, son of the dawn!
            You have been cut down to the earth,
            You who have weakened the nations!

13   "But you said in your heart,
            'I will ascend to heaven;
            I will raise my throne above the stars of God,
            And I will sit on the mount of assembly
            In the recesses of the north.

14   'I will ascend above the heights of the clouds;
            I will make myself like the Most High.'

15   "Nevertheless you will be thrust down to Sheol,
            To the recesses of the pit.

16   "Those who see you will gaze at you,
            They will ponder over you, *saying*,
            'Is this the man who made the earth tremble,
            Who shook kingdoms,

17   Who made the world like a wilderness
            And overthrew its cities,
            Who did not allow his prisoners to *go* home?'

18   "All the kings of the nations lie in glory,
            Each in his own tomb.

19   "But you have been cast out of your tomb
            Like a rejected branch,
            Clothed with the slain who are pierced with a sword,
            Who go down to the stones of the pit
            Like a trampled corpse.

20   "You will not be united with them in burial,
            Because you have ruined your country,
            You have slain your people.
            May the offspring of evildoers not be mentioned forever.

21   "Prepare for his sons a place of slaughter
            Because of the iniquity of their fathers.
            They must not arise and take possession of the earth
            And fill the face of the world with cities."

22   "I will rise up against them," declares the LORD of hosts, "and will cut off from Babylon
        name and survivors, offspring and posterity," declares the LORD.

23 "I will also make it a possession for the hedgehog and swamps of water, and I will sweep it with the broom of destruction," declares the LORD of hosts.

24 The LORD of hosts has sworn saying, "Surely, just as I have intended so it has happened, and just as I have planned so it will stand,

25 to break Assyria in My land, and I will trample him on My mountains. Then his yoke will be removed from them and his burden removed from their shoulder.

26 "This is the plan devised against the whole earth; and this is the hand that is stretched out against all the nations.

27 "For the LORD of hosts has planned, and who can frustrate *it?* And as for His stretched-out hand, who can turn it back?"

28 In the year that King Ahaz died this oracle came:

29   "Do not rejoice, O Philistia, all of you,

    Because the rod that struck you is broken;

    For from the serpent's root a viper will come out,

    And its fruit will be a flying serpent.

30   "Those who are most helpless will eat,

    And the needy will lie down in security;

    I will destroy your root with famine,

    And it will kill off your survivors.

31   "Wail, O gate; cry, O city;

    Melt away, O Philistia, all of you;

    For smoke comes from the north,

    And there is no straggler in his ranks.

32   "How then will one answer the messengers of the nation?

    That the LORD has founded Zion,

    And the afflicted of His people will seek refuge in it."

ISAIAH 15
Observation Worksheet

Chapter Theme _____

THE oracle concerning Moab.

    Surely in a night Ar of Moab is devastated *and* ruined;

    Surely in a night Kir of Moab is devastated *and* ruined.

2   They have gone up to the temple and *to* Dibon, *even* to the high places to weep.

    Moab wails over Nebo and Medeba;

    Everyone's head is bald *and* every beard is cut off.

3   In their streets they have girded themselves with sackcloth;

    On their housetops and in their squares

    Everyone is wailing, dissolved in tears.

4   Heshbon and Elealeh also cry out,

    Their voice is heard all the way to Jahaz;

    Therefore the armed men of Moab cry aloud;

    His soul trembles within him.

5   My heart cries out for Moab;

    His fugitives are as far as Zoar *and* Eglath-shelishiyah,

    For they go up the ascent of Luhith weeping;

    Surely on the road to Horonaim they raise a cry of distress over *their* ruin.

6   For the waters of Nimrim are desolate.

    Surely the grass is withered, the tender grass died out,

    There is no green thing.

7   Therefore the abundance *which* they have acquired and stored up

    They carry off over the brook of Arabim.

8   For the cry of distress has gone around the territory of Moab,

    Its wail *goes* as far as Eglaim and its wailing even to Beer-elim.

9   For the waters of Dimon are full of blood;

    Surely I will bring added *woes* upon Dimon,

    A lion upon the fugitives of Moab and upon the remnant of the land.

ISAIAH 16
Observation Worksheet

Chapter Theme _____

SEND the *tribute* lamb to the ruler of the land,

From Sela by way of the wilderness to the mountain of the daughter of Zion.

2 Then, like fleeing birds *or* scattered nestlings,

The daughters of Moab will be at the fords of the Arnon.

3 "Give *us* advice, make a decision;

Cast your shadow like night at high noon;

Hide the outcasts, do not betray the fugitive.

4 "Let the outcasts of Moab stay with you;

Be a hiding place to them from the destroyer."

For the extortioner has come to an end, destruction has ceased,

Oppressors have completely *disappeared* from the land.

5 A throne will even be established in lovingkindness,

And a judge will sit on it in faithfulness in the tent of David;

Moreover, he will seek justice

And be prompt in righteousness.

6 We have heard of the pride of Moab, an excessive pride;

Even of his arrogance, pride, and fury;

His idle boasts are false.

7 Therefore Moab will wail; everyone of Moab will wail.

You will moan for the raisin cakes of Kir-hareseth

As those who are utterly stricken.

8 For the fields of Heshbon have withered, the vines of Sibmah *as well;*

The lords of the nations have trampled down its choice clusters

Which reached as far as Jazer *and* wandered to the deserts;

Its tendrils spread themselves out *and* passed over the sea.

9 Therefore I will weep bitterly for Jazer, for the vine of Sibmah;

I will drench you with my tears, O Heshbon and Elealeh;

For the shouting over your summer fruits and your harvest has fallen away.

10   Gladness and joy are taken away from the fruitful field;
       In the vineyards also there will be no cries of joy or jubilant shouting,
       No treader treads out wine in the presses,
       For I have made the shouting to cease.

11   Therefore my heart intones like a harp for Moab
       And my inward feelings for Kir-hareseth.

12   So it will come about when Moab presents himself,
       When he wearies himself upon *his* high place
       And comes to his sanctuary to pray,
       That he will not prevail.

13   This is the word which the LORD spoke earlier concerning Moab.

14   But now the LORD speaks, saying, "Within three years, as a hired man would count them, the glory of Moab will be degraded along with all *his* great population, and *his* remnant will be very small *and* impotent."

ISAIAH 17
Observation Worksheet

Chapter Theme _____

THE oracle concerning Damascus.

"Behold, Damascus is about to be removed from being a city
And will become a fallen ruin.

2 "The cities of Aroer are forsaken;
They will be for flocks to lie down in,
And there will be no one to frighten *them*.

3 "The fortified city will disappear from Ephraim,
And sovereignty from Damascus
And the remnant of Aram;
They will be like the glory of the sons of Israel,"
Declares the LORD of hosts.

4 Now in that day the glory of Jacob will fade,
And the fatness of his flesh will become lean.

5 It will be even like the reaper gathering the standing grain,
As his arm harvests the ears,
Or it will be like one gleaning ears of grain
In the valley of Rephaim.

6 Yet gleanings will be left in it like the shaking of an olive tree,
Two *or* three olives on the topmost bough,
Four *or* five on the branches of a fruitful tree,
Declares the LORD, the God of Israel.

7 In that day man will have regard for his Maker
And his eyes will look to the Holy One of Israel.

8 He will not have regard for the altars, the work of his hands,
Nor will he look to that which his fingers have made,
Even the Asherim and incense stands.

9 In that day their strong cities will be like forsaken places in the forest,
Or like branches which they abandoned before the sons of Israel;
And the land will be a desolation.

10   For you have forgotten the God of your salvation
      And have not remembered the rock of your refuge.
      Therefore you plant delightful plants
      And set them with vine slips of a strange *god*.

11   In the day that you plant *it* you carefully fence *it* in,
      And in the morning you bring your seed to blossom;
      But the harvest will *be* a heap
      In a day of sickliness and incurable pain.

12   Alas, the uproar of many peoples
      Who roar like the roaring of the seas,
      And the rumbling of nations
      Who rush on like the rumbling of mighty waters!

13   The nations rumble on like the rumbling of many waters,
      But He will rebuke them and they will flee far away,
      And be chased like chaff in the mountains before the wind,
      Or like whirling dust before a gale.

14   At evening time, behold, *there is* terror!
      Before morning they are no more.
      Such *will be* the portion of those who plunder us
      And the lot of those who pillage us.

ISAIAH 18
Observation Worksheet

Chapter Theme _____

ALAS, oh land of whirring wings
      Which lies beyond the rivers of Cush,
2   Which sends envoys by the sea,
      Even in papyrus vessels on the surface of the waters.
      Go, swift messengers, to a nation tall and smooth,
      To a people feared far and wide,
      A powerful and oppressive nation
      Whose land the rivers divide.
3   All you inhabitants of the world and dwellers on earth,
      As soon as a standard is raised on the mountains, you will see *it*,
      And as soon as the trumpet is blown, you will hear *it*.
4   For thus the Lord has told me,
     "I will look from My dwelling place quietly
      Like dazzling heat in the sunshine,
      Like a cloud of dew in the heat of harvest."
5   For before the harvest, as soon as the bud blossoms
      And the flower becomes a ripening grape,
      Then He will cut off the sprigs with pruning knives
      And remove *and* cut away the spreading branches.
6   They will be left together for mountain birds of prey,
      And for the beasts of the earth;
      And the birds of prey will spend the summer *feeding* on them,
      And all the beasts of the earth will spend harvest time on them.
7   At that time a gift of homage will be brought to the Lord of hosts
      From a people tall and smooth,
      Even from a people feared far and wide,
      A powerful and oppressive nation,
      Whose land the rivers divide—
      To the place of the name of the Lord of hosts, *even* Mount Zion.

ISAIAH 19
Observation Worksheet

Chapter Theme _____

THE oracle concerning Egypt.

Behold, the Lord is riding on a swift cloud and is about to come to Egypt;

The idols of Egypt will tremble at His presence,

And the heart of the Egyptians will melt within them.

2 "So I will incite Egyptians against Egyptians;

And they will each fight against his brother and each against his neighbor,

City against city *and* kingdom against kingdom.

3 "Then the spirit of the Egyptians will be demoralized within them;

And I will confound their strategy,

So that they will resort to idols and ghosts of the dead

And to mediums and spiritists.

4 "Moreover, I will deliver the Egyptians into the hand of a cruel master,

And a mighty king will rule over them," declares the Lord God of hosts.

5 The waters from the sea will dry up,

And the river will be parched and dry.

6 The canals will emit a stench,

The streams of Egypt will thin out and dry up;

The reeds and rushes will rot away.

7 The bulrushes by the Nile, by the edge of the Nile

And all the sown fields by the Nile

Will become dry, be driven away, and be no more.

8 And the fishermen will lament,

And all those who cast a line into the Nile will mourn,

And those who spread nets on the waters will pine away.

9 Moreover, the manufacturers of linen made from combed flax

And the weavers of white cloth will be utterly dejected.

10 And the pillars *of Egypt* will be crushed;

All the hired laborers will be grieved in soul.

11   The princes of Zoan are mere fools;

      The advice of Pharaoh's wisest advisers has become stupid.

      How can you *men* say to Pharaoh,

      "I am a son of the wise, a son of ancient kings"?

12   Well then, where are your wise men?

      Please let them tell you,

      And let them understand what the Lord of hosts

      Has purposed against Egypt.

13   The princes of Zoan have acted foolishly,

      The princes of Memphis are deluded;

      Those who are the cornerstone of her tribes

      Have led Egypt astray.

14   The Lord has mixed within her a spirit of distortion;

      They have led Egypt astray in all that it does,

      As a drunken man staggers in his vomit.

15   There will be no work for Egypt

      Which *its* head or tail, *its* palm branch or bulrush, may do.

16   In that day the Egyptians will become like women, and they will tremble and be in dread because of the waving of the hand of the Lord of hosts, which He is going to wave over them.

17   The land of Judah will become a terror to Egypt; everyone to whom it is mentioned will be in dread of it, because of the purpose of the Lord of hosts which He is purposing against them.

18   In that day five cities in the land of Egypt will be speaking the language of Canaan and swearing *allegiance* to the Lord of hosts; one will be called the City of Destruction.

19   In that day there will be an altar to the Lord in the midst of the land of Egypt, and a pillar to the Lord near its border.

20   It will become a sign and a witness to the Lord of hosts in the land of Egypt; for they will cry to the Lord because of oppressors, and He will send them a Savior and a Champion, and He will deliver them.

21   Thus the Lord will make Himself known to Egypt, and the Egyptians will know the Lord in that day. They will even worship with sacrifice and offering, and will make a vow to the Lord and perform it.

22   The Lord will strike Egypt, striking but healing; so they will return to the Lord, and He will respond to them and will heal them.

23 In that day there will be a highway from Egypt to Assyria, and the Assyrians will come into Egypt and the Egyptians into Assyria, and the Egyptians will worship with the Assyrians.

24 In that day Israel will be the third *party* with Egypt and Assyria, a blessing in the midst of the earth,

25 whom the Lord of hosts has blessed, saying, "Blessed is Egypt My people, and Assyria the work of My hands, and Israel My inheritance."

ISAIAH 20
Observation Worksheet

Chapter Theme _____

IN the year that the commander came to Ashdod, when Sargon the king of Assyria sent him and he fought against Ashdod and captured it,

2   at that time the LORD spoke through Isaiah the son of Amoz, saying, "Go and loosen the sackcloth from your hips and take your shoes off your feet." And he did so, going naked and barefoot.

3   And the LORD said, "Even as My servant Isaiah has gone naked and barefoot three years as a sign and token against Egypt and Cush,

4   so the king of Assyria will lead away the captives of Egypt and the exiles of Cush, young and old, naked and barefoot with buttocks uncovered, to the shame of Egypt.

5   "Then they will be dismayed and ashamed because of Cush their hope and Egypt their boast.

6   "So the inhabitants of this coastland will say in that day, 'Behold, such is our hope, where we fled for help to be delivered from the king of Assyria; and we, how shall we escape?' "

ISAIAH 21
Observation Worksheet

Chapter Theme _____

THE oracle concerning the wilderness of the sea.

> As windstorms in the Negev sweep on,
>
> It comes from the wilderness, from a terrifying land.

2   A harsh vision has been shown to me;

> The treacherous one *still* deals treacherously, and the destroyer *still* destroys.
>
> Go up, Elam, lay siege, Media;
>
> I have made an end of all the groaning she has caused.

3   For this reason my loins are full of anguish;

> Pains have seized me like the pains of a woman in labor.
>
> I am so bewildered I cannot hear, so terrified I cannot see.

4   My mind reels, horror overwhelms me;

> The twilight I longed for has been turned for me into trembling.

5   They set the table, they spread out the cloth, they eat, they drink;

> "Rise up, captains, oil the shields,"

6   For thus the Lord says to me,

> "Go, station the lookout, let him report what he sees.

7   "When he sees riders, horsemen in pairs,

> A train of donkeys, a train of camels,
>
> Let him pay close attention, very close attention."

8   Then the lookout called,

> "O Lord, I stand continually by day on the watchtower,
>
> And I am stationed every night at my guard post.

9   "Now behold, here comes a troop of riders, horsemen in pairs."

> And one said, "Fallen, fallen is Babylon;
>
> And all the images of her gods are shattered on the ground."

10   O my threshed *people,* and my afflicted of the threshing floor!

> What I have heard from the LORD of hosts,
>
> The God of Israel, I make known to you.

11   The oracle concerning Edom.

        One keeps calling to me from Seir,

      "Watchman, how far gone is the night?

        Watchman, how far gone is the night?"

12   The watchman says,

      "Morning comes but also night.

        If you would inquire, inquire;

        Come back again."

13   The oracle about Arabia.

        In the thickets of Arabia you must spend the night,

        O caravans of Dedanites.

14   Bring water for the thirsty,

        O inhabitants of the land of Tema,

        Meet the fugitive with bread.

15   For they have fled from the swords,

        From the drawn sword, and from the bent bow

        And from the press of battle.

16   For thus the Lord said to me, "In a year, as a hired man would count it, all the splendor of Kedar will terminate;

17   and the remainder of the number of bowmen, the mighty men of the sons of Kedar, will be few; for the LORD God of Israel has spoken."

ISAIAH 22
Observation Worksheet

Chapter Theme _____

THE oracle concerning the valley of vision.

What is the matter with you now, that you have all gone up to the housetops?

2   You who were full of noise,

You boisterous town, you exultant city;

Your slain were not slain with the sword,

Nor did they die in battle.

3   All your rulers have fled together,

And have been captured without the bow;

All of you who were found were taken captive together,

Though they had fled far away.

4   Therefore I say, "Turn your eyes away from me,

Let me weep bitterly,

Do not try to comfort me concerning the destruction of the daughter of my people."

5   For the Lord GOD of hosts has a day of panic, subjugation and confusion

In the valley of vision,

A breaking down of walls

And a crying to the mountain.

6   Elam took up the quiver

With the chariots, infantry *and* horsemen;

And Kir uncovered the shield.

7   Then your choicest valleys were full of chariots,

And the horsemen took up fixed positions at the gate.

8   And He removed the defense of Judah.

In that day you depended on the weapons of the house of the forest,

9   And you saw that the breaches

In the *wall* of the city of David were many;

And you collected the waters of the lower pool.

10   Then you counted the houses of Jerusalem

And tore down houses to fortify the wall.

11   And you made a reservoir between the two walls

For the waters of the old pool.

But you did not depend on Him who made it,

Nor did you take into consideration Him who planned it long ago.

12   Therefore in that day the Lord GOD of hosts called *you* to weeping, to wailing,

To shaving the head and to wearing sackcloth.

13   Instead, there is gaiety and gladness,

Killing of cattle and slaughtering of sheep,

Eating of meat and drinking of wine:

"Let us eat and drink, for tomorrow we may die."

14   But the LORD of hosts revealed Himself to me,

"Surely this iniquity shall not be forgiven you

Until you die," says the Lord GOD of hosts.

15   Thus says the Lord GOD of hosts,

"Come, go to this steward,

To Shebna, who is in charge of the *royal* household,

16   'What right do you have here,

And whom do you have here,

That you have hewn a tomb for yourself here,

You who hew a tomb on the height,

You who carve a resting place for yourself in the rock?

17   'Behold, the LORD is about to hurl you headlong, O man.

And He is about to grasp you firmly

18   *And* roll you tightly like a ball,

To be cast into a vast country;

There you will die

And there your splendid chariots will be,

You shame of your master's house.'

19   "I will depose you from your office,

And I will pull you down from your station.

20   "Then it will come about in that day,

That I will summon My servant Eliakim the son of Hilkiah,

21   And I will clothe him with your tunic

And tie your sash securely about him.

I will entrust him with your authority,

And he will become a father to the inhabitants of Jerusalem and to the house of Judah.

22   "Then I will set the key of the house of David on his shoulder,

When he opens no one will shut,

When he shuts no one will open.

23   "I will drive him *like* a peg in a firm place,

And he will become a throne of glory to his father's house.

24   "So they will hang on him all the glory of his father's house, offspring and issue, all the least of vessels, from bowls to all the jars.

25   "In that day," declares the Lord of hosts, "the peg driven in a firm place will give way; it will even break off and fall, and the load hanging on it will be cut off, for the Lord has spoken."

ISAIAH 23
Observation Worksheet

Chapter Theme _____

THE oracle concerning Tyre.

Wail, O ships of Tarshish,

For *Tyre* is destroyed, without house *or* harbor;

It is reported to them from the land of Cyprus.

2   Be silent, you inhabitants of the coastland,

You merchants of Sidon;

Your messengers crossed the sea

3   And *were* on many waters.

The grain of the Nile, the harvest of the River was her revenue;

And she was the market of nations.

4   Be ashamed, O Sidon;

For the sea speaks, the stronghold of the sea, saying,

"I have neither travailed nor given birth,

I have neither brought up young men *nor* reared virgins."

5   When the report *reaches* Egypt,

They will be in anguish at the report of Tyre.

6   Pass over to Tarshish;

Wail, O inhabitants of the coastland.

7   Is this your jubilant *city*,

Whose origin is from antiquity,

Whose feet used to carry her to colonize distant places?

8   Who has planned this against Tyre, the bestower of crowns,

Whose merchants were princes, whose traders were the honored of the earth?

9   The Lord of hosts has planned it, to defile the pride of all beauty,

To despise all the honored of the earth.

10   Overflow your land like the Nile, O daughter of Tarshish,

There is no more restraint.

11   He has stretched His hand out over the sea,

He has made the kingdoms tremble;

The Lord has given a command concerning Canaan to demolish its strongholds.

12   He has said, "You shall exult no more, O crushed virgin daughter of Sidon.

Arise, pass over to Cyprus; even there you will find no rest."

13   Behold, the land of the Chaldeans—this is the people *which* was not; Assyria appointed it for desert creatures—they erected their siege towers, they stripped its palaces, they made it a ruin.

14   Wail, O ships of Tarshish,

For your stronghold is destroyed.

15   Now in that day Tyre will be forgotten for seventy years like the days of one king. At the end of seventy years it will happen to Tyre as *in* the song of the harlot:

16   Take *your* harp, walk about the city,

O forgotten harlot;

Pluck the strings skillfully, sing many songs,

That you may be remembered.

17   It will come about at the end of seventy years that the Lord will visit Tyre. Then she will go back to her harlot's wages and will play the harlot with all the kingdoms on the face of the earth.

18   Her gain and her harlot's wages will be set apart to the Lord; it will not be stored up or hoarded, but her gain will become sufficient food and choice attire for those who dwell in the presence of the Lord.

ISAIAH 24
Observation Worksheet

Chapter Theme _____

BEHOLD, the LORD lays the earth waste, devastates it, distorts its surface and scatters its inhabitants.

2 And the people will be like the priest, the servant like his master, the maid like her mistress, the buyer like the seller, the lender like the borrower, the creditor like the debtor.

3 The earth will be completely laid waste and completely despoiled, for the LORD has spoken this word.

4 The earth mourns *and* withers, the world fades *and* withers, the exalted of the people of the earth fade away.

5 The earth is also polluted by its inhabitants, for they transgressed laws, violated statutes, broke the everlasting covenant.

6 Therefore, a curse devours the earth, and those who live in it are held guilty. Therefore, the inhabitants of the earth are burned, and few men are left.

7 The new wine mourns,
The vine decays,
All the merry-hearted sigh.

8 The gaiety of tambourines ceases,
The noise of revelers stops,
The gaiety of the harp ceases.

9 They do not drink wine with song;
Strong drink is bitter to those who drink it.

10 The city of chaos is broken down;
Every house is shut up so that none may enter.

11 There is an outcry in the streets concerning the wine;
All joy turns to gloom.
The gaiety of the earth is banished.

12 Desolation is left in the city
And the gate is battered to ruins.

13   For thus it will be in the midst of the earth among the peoples,

As the shaking of an olive tree,

As the gleanings when the grape harvest is over.

14   They raise their voices, they shout for joy;

They cry out from the west concerning the majesty of the LORD.

15   Therefore glorify the LORD in the east,

The name of the LORD, the God of Israel,

In the coastlands of the sea.

16   From the ends of the earth we hear songs, "Glory to the Righteous One,"

But I say, "Woe to me! Woe to me! Alas for me!

The treacherous deal treacherously,

And the treacherous deal very treacherously."

17   Terror and pit and snare

Confront you, O inhabitant of the earth.

18   Then it will be that he who flees the report of disaster will fall into the pit,

And he who climbs out of the pit will be caught in the snare;

For the windows above are opened, and the foundations of the earth shake.

19   The earth is broken asunder,

The earth is split through,

The earth is shaken violently.

20   The earth reels to and fro like a drunkard

And it totters like a shack,

For its transgression is heavy upon it,

And it will fall, never to rise again.

21   So it will happen in that day,

That the LORD will punish the host of heaven on high,

And the kings of the earth on earth.

22   They will be gathered together

Like prisoners in the dungeon,

And will be confined in prison;

And after many days they *will be* punished.

23   Then the moon will be abashed and the sun ashamed,

For the LORD of hosts will reign on Mount Zion and in Jerusalem,

And *His* glory will be before His elders.

ISAIAH 25
Observation Worksheet

Chapter Theme _____

O LORD, You are my God;

    I will exalt You, I will give thanks to Your name;

    For You have worked wonders,

    Plans *formed* long ago, with perfect faithfulness.

2   For You have made a city into a heap,

    A fortified city into a ruin;

    A palace of strangers is a city no more,

    It will never be rebuilt.

3   Therefore a strong people will glorify You;

    Cities of ruthless nations will revere You.

4   For You have been a defense for the helpless,

    A defense for the needy in his distress,

    A refuge from the storm, a shade from the heat;

    For the breath of the ruthless

    Is like a *rain* storm *against* a wall.

5   Like heat in drought, You subdue the uproar of aliens;

    Like heat by the shadow of a cloud, the song of the ruthless is silenced.

6   The LORD of hosts will prepare a lavish banquet for all peoples on this mountain;

    A banquet of aged wine, choice pieces with marrow,

    And refined, aged wine.

7   And on this mountain He will swallow up the covering which is over all peoples,

    Even the veil which is stretched over all nations.

8   He will swallow up death for all time,

    And the Lord GOD will wipe tears away from all faces,

    And He will remove the reproach of His people from all the earth;

    For the LORD has spoken.

9   And it will be said in that day,

    "Behold, this is our God for whom we have waited that He might save us.

    This is the LORD for whom we have waited;

    Let us rejoice and be glad in His salvation."

10   For the hand of the LORD will rest on this mountain,
     And Moab will be trodden down in his place
     As straw is trodden down in the water of a manure pile.
11   And he will spread out his hands in the middle of it
     As a swimmer spreads out *his hands* to swim,
     But *the Lord* will lay low his pride together with the trickery of his hands.
12   The unassailable fortifications of your walls He will bring down,
     Lay low *and* cast to the ground, even to the dust.

ISAIAH 26
Observation Worksheet

Chapter Theme _____

IN that day this song will be sung in the land of Judah:
> "We have a strong city;
> He sets up walls and ramparts for security.

2   "Open the gates, that the righteous nation may enter,
> The one that remains faithful.

3   "The steadfast of mind You will keep in perfect peace,
> Because he trusts in You.

4   "Trust in the LORD forever,
> For in GOD the LORD, *we have* an everlasting Rock.

5   "For He has brought low those who dwell on high, the unassailable city;
> He lays it low, He lays it low to the ground, He casts it to the dust.

6   "The foot will trample it,
> The feet of the afflicted, the steps of the helpless."

7   The way of the righteous is smooth;
> O Upright One, make the path of the righteous level.

8   Indeed, *while following* the way of Your judgments, O LORD,
> We have waited for You eagerly;
> Your name, even Your memory, is the desire of *our* souls.

9   At night my soul longs for You,
> Indeed, my spirit within me seeks You diligently;
> For when the earth experiences Your judgments
> The inhabitants of the world learn righteousness.

10   *Though* the wicked is shown favor,
> He does not learn righteousness;
> He deals unjustly in the land of uprightness,
> And does not perceive the majesty of the LORD.

11   O LORD, Your hand is lifted up *yet* they do not see it.
> They see *Your* zeal for the people and are put to shame;
> Indeed, fire will devour Your enemies.

12   LORD, You will establish peace for us,
> Since You have also performed for us all our works.

13   O Lord our God, other masters besides You have ruled us;
      But through You alone we confess Your name.

14   The dead will not live, the departed spirits will not rise;
      Therefore You have punished and destroyed them,
      And You have wiped out all remembrance of them.

15   You have increased the nation, O Lord,
      You have increased the nation, You are glorified;
      You have extended all the borders of the land.

16   O Lord, they sought You in distress;
      They could only whisper a prayer,
      Your chastening was upon them.

17   As the pregnant woman approaches *the time* to give birth,
      She writhes *and* cries out in her labor pains,
      Thus were we before You, O Lord.

18   We were pregnant, we writhed *in labor*,
      We gave birth, as it seems, *only* to wind.
      We could not accomplish deliverance for the earth,
      Nor were inhabitants of the world born.

19   Your dead will live;
      Their corpses will rise.
      You who lie in the dust, awake and shout for joy,
      For your dew *is as* the dew of the dawn,
      And the earth will give birth to the departed spirits.

20   Come, my people, enter into your rooms
      And close your doors behind you;
      Hide for a little while
      Until indignation runs *its* course.

21   For behold, the Lord is about to come out from His place
      To punish the inhabitants of the earth for their iniquity;
      And the earth will reveal her bloodshed
      And will no longer cover her slain.

ISAIAH 27
Observation Worksheet

Chapter Theme _____

IN that day the LORD will punish Leviathan the fleeing serpent,

    With His fierce and great and mighty sword,

    Even Leviathan the twisted serpent;

    And He will kill the dragon who *lives* in the sea.

2   In that day,

    "A vineyard of wine, sing of it!

3   "I, the LORD, am its keeper;

    I water it every moment.

    So that no one will damage it,

    I guard it night and day.

4   "I have no wrath.

    Should someone give Me briars *and* thorns in battle,

    Then I would step on them, I would burn them completely.

5   "Or let him rely on My protection,

    Let him make peace with Me,

    Let him make peace with Me."

6   In the days to come Jacob will take root,

    Israel will blossom and sprout,

    And they will fill the whole world with fruit.

7   Like the striking of Him who has struck them, has He struck them?

    Or like the slaughter of His slain, have they been slain?

8   You contended with them by banishing them, by driving them away.

    With His fierce wind He has expelled *them* on the day of the east wind.

9   Therefore through this Jacob's iniquity will be forgiven;

    And this will be the full price of the pardoning of his sin:

    When he makes all the altar stones like pulverized chalk stones;

    When Asherim and incense altars will not stand.

10   For the fortified city is isolated,
A homestead forlorn and forsaken like the desert;
There the calf will graze,
And there it will lie down and feed on its branches.

11   When its limbs are dry, they are broken off;
Women come *and* make a fire with them,
For they are not a people of discernment,
Therefore their Maker will not have compassion on them.
And their Creator will not be gracious to them.

12   In that day the Lord will start *His* threshing from the flowing stream of the Euphrates to the brook of Egypt, and you will be gathered up one by one, O sons of Israel.

13   It will come about also in that day that a great trumpet will be blown, and those who were perishing in the land of Assyria and who were scattered in the land of Egypt will come and worship the Lord in the holy mountain at Jerusalem.

ISAIAH 28
Observation Worksheet

Chapter Theme _____

WOE to the proud crown of the drunkards of Ephraim,

    And to the fading flower of its glorious beauty,

    Which is at the head of the fertile valley

    Of those who are overcome with wine!

2   Behold, the Lord has a strong and mighty *agent;*

    As a storm of hail, a tempest of destruction,

    Like a storm of mighty overflowing waters,

    He has cast *it* down to the earth with *His* hand.

3   The proud crown of the drunkards of Ephraim is trodden under foot.

4   And the fading flower of its glorious beauty,

    Which is at the head of the fertile valley,

    Will be like the first-ripe fig prior to summer,

    Which one sees,

    And as soon as it is in his hand,

    He swallows it.

5   In that day the LORD of hosts will become a beautiful crown

    And a glorious diadem to the remnant of His people;

6   A spirit of justice for him who sits in judgment,

    A strength to those who repel the onslaught at the gate.

7   And these also reel with wine and stagger from strong drink:

    The priest and the prophet reel with strong drink,

    They are confused by wine, they stagger from strong drink;

    They reel while having visions,

    They totter *when rendering* judgment.

8   For all the tables are full of filthy vomit, without a *single clean* place.

9   "To whom would He teach knowledge,

    And to whom would He interpret the message?

    Those *just* weaned from milk?

    Those *just* taken from the breast?

10   "For *He says,*

        'Order on order, order on order,

        Line on line, line on line,

        A little here, a little there.' "

11   Indeed, He will speak to this people

        Through stammering lips and a foreign tongue,

12   He who said to them, "Here is rest, give rest to the weary,"

        And, "Here is repose," but they would not listen.

13   So the word of the LORD to them will be,

        "Order on order, order on order,

        Line on line, line on line,

        A little here, a little there,"

        That they may go and stumble backward, be broken, snared and taken captive.

14   Therefore, hear the word of the LORD, O scoffers,

        Who rule this people who are in Jerusalem,

15   Because you have said, "We have made a covenant with death,

        And with Sheol we have made a pact.

        The overwhelming scourge will not reach us when it passes by,

        For we have made falsehood our refuge and we have concealed ourselves with deception."

16   Therefore thus says the Lord GOD,

        "Behold, I am laying in Zion a stone, a tested stone,

        A costly cornerstone *for* the foundation, firmly placed.

        He who believes *in it* will not be disturbed.

17   "I will make justice the measuring line

        And righteousness the level;

        Then hail will sweep away the refuge of lies

        And the waters will overflow the secret place.

18   "Your covenant with death will be canceled,

        And your pact with Sheol will not stand;

        When the overwhelming scourge passes through,

        Then you become its trampling *place.*

19   "As often as it passes through, it will seize you;

        For morning after morning it will pass through, *anytime* during the day or night,

        And it will be sheer terror to understand what it means."

20   The bed is too short on which to stretch out,

        And the blanket is too small to wrap oneself in.

21   For the LORD will rise up as *at* Mount Perazim,
      He will be stirred up as in the valley of Gibeon,
      To do His task, His unusual task,
      And to work His work, His extraordinary work.

22   And now do not carry on as scoffers,
      Or your fetters will be made stronger;
      For I have heard from the Lord GOD of hosts
      Of decisive destruction on all the earth.

23 Give ear and hear my voice,
      Listen and hear my words.

24   Does the farmer plow continually to plant seed?
      Does he *continually* turn and harrow the ground?

25   Does he not level its surface
      And sow dill and scatter cummin
      And plant wheat in rows,
      Barley in its place and rye within its area?

26   For his God instructs and teaches him properly.

27   For dill is not threshed with a threshing sledge,
      Nor is the cartwheel driven over cummin;
      But dill is beaten out with a rod, and cummin with a club.

28   *Grain for* bread is crushed,
      Indeed, he does not continue to thresh it forever.
      Because the wheel of *his* cart and his horses *eventually* damage *it,*
      He does not thresh it longer.

29   This also comes from the LORD of hosts,
      Who has made *His* counsel wonderful and *His* wisdom great.

Observation Worksheet

Chapter Theme _____

WOE, O Ariel, Ariel the city *where* David *once* camped!

      Add year to year, observe *your* feasts on schedule.

2   I will bring distress to Ariel,

      And she will be *a city of* lamenting and mourning;

      And she will be like an Ariel to me.

3   I will camp against you encircling *you,*

      And I will set siegeworks against you,

      And I will raise up battle towers against you.

4   Then you will be brought low;

      From the earth you will speak,

      And from the dust *where* you are prostrate

      Your words *will come.*

      Your voice will also be like that of a spirit from the ground,

      And your speech will whisper from the dust.

5   But the multitude of your enemies will become like fine dust,

      And the multitude of the ruthless ones like the chaff which blows away;

      And it will happen instantly, suddenly.

6   From the Lord of hosts you will be punished with thunder and earthquake and loud noise,

      With whirlwind and tempest and the flame of a consuming fire.

7   And the multitude of all the nations who wage war against Ariel,

      Even all who wage war against her and her stronghold, and who distress her,

      Will be like a dream, a vision of the night.

8   It will be as when a hungry man dreams—

      And behold, he is eating;

      But when he awakens, his hunger is not satisfied,

      Or as when a thirsty man dreams—

      And behold, he is drinking,

      But when he awakens, behold, he is faint

And his thirst is not quenched.
Thus the multitude of all the nations will be
Who wage war against Mount Zion.

9   Be delayed and wait,
Blind yourselves and be blind;
They become drunk, but not with wine,
They stagger, but not with strong drink.

10   For the LORD has poured over you a spirit of deep sleep,
He has shut your eyes, the prophets;
And He has covered your heads, the seers.

11   The entire vision will be to you like the words of a sealed book, which when they give it to the one who is literate, saying, "Please read this," he will say, "I cannot, for it is sealed."

12   Then the book will be given to the one who is illiterate, saying, "Please read this." And he will say, "I cannot read."

13   Then the Lord said,
"Because this people draw near with their words
And honor Me with their lip service,
But they remove their hearts far from Me,
And their reverence for Me consists of tradition learned *by rote,*

14   Therefore behold, I will once again deal marvelously with this people, wondrously marvelous;
And the wisdom of their wise men will perish,
And the discernment of their discerning men will be concealed."

15   Woe to those who deeply hide their plans from the LORD,
And whose deeds are *done* in a dark place,
And they say, "Who sees us?" or "Who knows us?"

16   You turn *things* around!
Shall the potter be considered as equal with the clay,
That what is made would say to its maker, "He did not make me";
Or what is formed say to him who formed it, "He has no understanding"?

17   Is it not yet just a little while
Before Lebanon will be turned into a fertile field,
And the fertile field will be considered as a forest?

18   On that day the deaf will hear words of a book,

And out of *their* gloom and darkness the eyes of the blind will see.

19   The afflicted also will increase their gladness in the LORD,

And the needy of mankind will rejoice in the Holy One of Israel.

20   For the ruthless will come to an end and the scorner will be finished,

Indeed all who are intent on doing evil will be cut off;

21   Who cause a person to be indicted by a word,

And ensnare him who adjudicates at the gate,

And defraud the one in the right with meaningless arguments.

22   Therefore thus says the LORD, who redeemed Abraham, concerning the house of Jacob:

"Jacob shall not now be ashamed, nor shall his face now turn pale;

23   But when he sees his children, the work of My hands, in his midst,

They will sanctify My name;

Indeed, they will sanctify the Holy One of Jacob

And will stand in awe of the God of Israel.

24   "Those who err in mind will know the truth,

And those who criticize will accept instruction.

Chapter Theme _____

"WOE to the rebellious children," declares the Lord,

    "Who execute a plan, but not Mine,

    And make an alliance, but not of My Spirit,

    In order to add sin to sin;

2   Who proceed down to Egypt

    Without consulting Me,

    To take refuge in the safety of Pharaoh

    And to seek shelter in the shadow of Egypt!

3   "Therefore the safety of Pharaoh will be your shame

    And the shelter in the shadow of Egypt, your humiliation.

4   "For their princes are at Zoan

    And their ambassadors arrive at Hanes.

5   "Everyone will be ashamed because of a people who cannot profit them,

    Who are not for help or profit, but for shame and also for reproach."

6   The oracle concerning the beasts of the Negev.

    Through a land of distress and anguish,

    From where *come* lioness and lion, viper and flying serpent,

    They carry their riches on the backs of young donkeys

    And their treasures on camels' humps,

    To a people who cannot profit *them;*

7   Even Egypt, whose help is vain and empty.

    Therefore, I have called her

    "Rahab who has been exterminated."

8   Now go, write it on a tablet before them

    And inscribe it on a scroll,

    That it may serve in the time to come

    As a witness forever.

9   For this is a rebellious people, false sons,

    Sons who refuse to listen

    To the instruction of the Lord;

10   Who say to the seers, "You must not see *visions*";
      And to the prophets, "You must not prophesy to us what is right,
      Speak to us pleasant words,
      Prophesy illusions.

11   "Get out of the way, turn aside from the path,
      Let us hear no more about the Holy One of Israel."

12   Therefore thus says the Holy One of Israel,
      "Since you have rejected this word
      And have put your trust in oppression and guile, and have relied on them,

13   Therefore this iniquity will be to you
      Like a breach about to fall,
      A bulge in a high wall,
      Whose collapse comes suddenly in an instant,

14   Whose collapse is like the smashing of a potter's jar,
      So ruthlessly shattered
      That a sherd will not be found among its pieces
      To take fire from a hearth
      Or to scoop water from a cistern."

15   For thus the Lord God, the Holy One of Israel, has said,
      "In repentance and rest you will be saved,
      In quietness and trust is your strength."
      But you were not willing,

16   And you said, "No, for we will flee on horses,"
      Therefore you shall flee!
      "And we will ride on swift *horses*,"
      Therefore those who pursue you shall be swift.

17   One thousand *will flee* at the threat of one *man*;
      You will flee at the threat of five,
      Until you are left as a flag on a mountain top
      And as a signal on a hill.

18   Therefore the LORD longs to be gracious to you,
      And therefore He waits on high to have compassion on you.
      For the LORD is a God of justice;
      How blessed are all those who long for Him.

19   O people in Zion, inhabitant in Jerusalem, you will weep no longer. He will surely be gracious to you at the sound of your cry; when He hears it, He will answer you.

20   Although the Lord has given you bread of privation and water of oppression, *He,* your Teacher will no longer hide Himself, but your eyes will behold your Teacher.

21   Your ears will hear a word behind you, "This is the way, walk in it," whenever you turn to the right or to the left.

22   And you will defile your graven images overlaid with silver, and your molten images plated with gold. You will scatter them as an impure thing, *and* say to them, "Be gone!"

23   Then He will give *you* rain for the seed which you will sow in the ground, and bread *from* the yield of the ground, and it will be rich and plenteous; on that day your livestock will graze in a roomy pasture.

24   Also the oxen and the donkeys which work the ground will eat salted fodder, which has been winnowed with shovel and fork.

25   On every lofty mountain and on every high hill there will be streams running with water on the day of the great slaughter, when the towers fall.

26   The light of the moon will be as the light of the sun, and the light of the sun will be seven times *brighter,* like the light of seven days, on the day the LORD binds up the fracture of His people and heals the bruise He has inflicted.

27   Behold, the name of the LORD comes from a remote place;
Burning is His anger and dense is *His* smoke;
His lips are filled with indignation
And His tongue is like a consuming fire;

28   His breath is like an overflowing torrent,
Which reaches to the neck,
To shake the nations back and forth in a sieve,
And to *put* in the jaws of the peoples the bridle which leads to ruin.

29   You will have songs as in the night when you keep the festival,
And gladness of heart as when one marches to *the sound of* the flute,
To go to the mountain of the LORD, to the Rock of Israel.

30   And the LORD will cause His voice of authority to be heard,
And the descending of His arm to be seen in fierce anger,
And *in* the flame of a consuming fire
In cloudburst, downpour and hailstones.

31   For at the voice of the LORD Assyria will be terrified,
When He strikes with the rod.

32 And every blow of the rod of punishment,

   Which the LORD will lay on him,

   Will be with *the music of* tambourines and lyres;

   And in battles, brandishing weapons, He will fight them.

33 For Topheth has long been ready,

   Indeed, it has been prepared for the king.

   He has made it deep and large,

   A pyre of fire with plenty of wood;

   The breath of the LORD, like a torrent of brimstone, sets it afire.

ISAIAH 31
Observation Worksheet

Chapter Theme _____

WOE to those who go down to Egypt for help

    And rely on horses,

    And trust in chariots because they are many

    And in horsemen because they are very strong,

    But they do not look to the Holy One of Israel, nor seek the LORD!

2   Yet He also is wise and will bring disaster

    And does not retract His words,

    But will arise against the house of evildoers

    And against the help of the workers of iniquity.

3   Now the Egyptians are men and not God,

    And their horses are flesh and not spirit;

    So the LORD will stretch out His hand,

    And he who helps will stumble

    And he who is helped will fall,

    And all of them will come to an end together.

4   For thus says the LORD to me,

    "As the lion or the young lion growls over his prey,

    Against which a band of shepherds is called out,

    And he will not be terrified at their voice nor disturbed at their noise,

    So will the LORD of hosts come down to wage war on Mount Zion and on its hill."

5   Like flying birds so the LORD of hosts will protect Jerusalem.

    He will protect and deliver *it*;

    He will pass over and rescue *it*.

6   Return to Him from whom you have deeply defected, O sons of Israel.

7   For in that day every man will cast away his silver idols and his gold idols, which your sinful hands have made for you as a sin.

8   And the Assyrian will fall by a sword not of man,

    And a sword not of man will devour him.

So he will not escape the sword,

And his young men will become forced laborers.

9   "His rock will pass away because of panic,

And his princes will be terrified at the standard,"

Declares the Lord, whose fire is in Zion and whose furnace is in Jerusalem.

ISAIAH 32
Observation Worksheet

Chapter Theme _____

BEHOLD, a king will reign righteously
     And princes will rule justly.
2   Each will be like a refuge from the wind
     And a shelter from the storm,
     Like streams of water in a dry country,
     Like the shade of a huge rock in a parched land.
3   Then the eyes of those who see will not be blinded,
     And the ears of those who hear will listen.
4   The mind of the hasty will discern the truth,
     And the tongue of the stammerers will hasten to speak clearly.
5   No longer will the fool be called noble,
     Or the rogue be spoken of *as* generous.
6   For a fool speaks nonsense,
     And his heart inclines toward wickedness:
     To practice ungodliness and to speak error against the Lord,
     To keep the hungry person unsatisfied
     And to withhold drink from the thirsty.
7   As for a rogue, his weapons are evil;
     He devises wicked schemes
     To destroy *the* afflicted with slander,
     Even though *the* needy one speaks what is right.
8   But the noble man devises noble plans;
     And by noble plans he stands.

9   Rise up, you women who are at ease,
     And hear my voice;
     Give ear to my word,
     You complacent daughters.
10   Within a year and *a few* days
     You will be troubled, O complacent *daughters;*

For the vintage is ended,

And the *fruit* gathering will not come.

11 Tremble, you *women* who are at ease;

Be troubled, you complacent *daughters;*

Strip, undress and put *sackcloth* on *your* waist,

12 Beat your breasts for the pleasant fields, for the fruitful vine,

13 For the land of my people *in which* thorns *and* briars shall come up;

Yea, for all the joyful houses *and for* the jubilant city.

14 Because the palace has been abandoned, the populated city forsaken.

Hill and watch-tower have become caves forever,

A delight for wild donkeys, a pasture for flocks;

15 Until the Spirit is poured out upon us from on high,

And the wilderness becomes a fertile field,

And the fertile field is considered as a forest.

16 Then justice will dwell in the wilderness

And righteousness will abide in the fertile field.

17 And the work of righteousness will be peace,

And the service of righteousness, quietness and confidence forever.

18 Then my people will live in a peaceful habitation,

And in secure dwellings and in undisturbed resting places;

19 And it will hail when the forest comes down,

And the city will be utterly laid low.

20 How blessed will you be, you who sow beside all waters,

Who let out freely the ox and the donkey.

ISAIAH 33
Observation Worksheet

Chapter Theme _____

WOE to you, O destroyer,

    While you were not destroyed;

    And he who is treacherous, while *others* did not deal treacherously with him.

    As soon as you finish destroying, you will be destroyed;

    As soon as you cease to deal treacherously, *others* will deal treacherously with you.

2   O Lord, be gracious to us; we have waited for You.

    Be their strength every morning,

    Our salvation also in the time of distress.

3   At the sound of the tumult peoples flee;

    At the lifting up of Yourself nations disperse.

4   Your spoil is gathered *as* the caterpillar gathers;

    As locusts rushing about men rush about on it.

5   The Lord is exalted, for He dwells on high;

    He has filled Zion with justice and righteousness.

6   And He will be the stability of your times,

    A wealth of salvation, wisdom and knowledge;

    The fear of the Lord is his treasure.

7   Behold, their brave men cry in the streets,

    The ambassadors of peace weep bitterly.

8   The highways are desolate, the traveler has ceased,

    He has broken the covenant, he has despised the cities,

    He has no regard for man.

9   The land mourns *and* pines away,

    Lebanon is shamed *and* withers;

    Sharon is like a desert plain,

    And Bashan and Carmel lose *their foliage.*

10   "Now I will arise," says the Lord,

    "Now I will be exalted, now I will be lifted up.

11   "You have conceived chaff, you will give birth to stubble;

    My breath will consume you like a fire.

12   "The peoples will be burned to lime,
        Like cut thorns which are burned in the fire.

13   "You who are far away, hear what I have done;
        And you who are near, acknowledge My might."

14   Sinners in Zion are terrified;
        Trembling has seized the godless.
      "Who among us can live with the consuming fire?
        Who among us can live with continual burning?"

15   He who walks righteously and speaks with sincerity,
        He who rejects unjust gain
        And shakes his hands so that they hold no bribe;
        He who stops his ears from hearing about bloodshed
        And shuts his eyes from looking upon evil;

16   He will dwell on the heights,
        His refuge will be the impregnable rock;
        His bread will be given *him,*
        His water will be sure.

17   Your eyes will see the King in His beauty;
        They will behold a far-distant land.

18   Your heart will meditate on terror:
      "Where is he who counts?
        Where is he who weighs?
        Where is he who counts the towers?"

19   You will no longer see a fierce people,
        A people of unintelligible speech which no one comprehends,
        Of a stammering tongue which no one understands.

20   Look upon Zion, the city of our appointed feasts;
        Your eyes will see Jerusalem, an undisturbed habitation,
        A tent which will not be folded;
        Its stakes will never be pulled up,
        Nor any of its cords be torn apart.

21   But there the majestic *One,* the LORD, will be for us
        A place of rivers *and* wide canals
        On which no boat with oars will go,
        And on which no mighty ship will pass—

22   For the LORD is our judge,
        The LORD is our lawgiver,
        The LORD is our king;
        He will save us—

23   Your tackle hangs slack;
        It cannot hold the base of its mast firmly,
        Nor spread out the sail.
        Then the prey of an abundant spoil will be divided;
        The lame will take the plunder.

24   And no resident will say, "I am sick";
        The people who dwell there will be forgiven *their* iniquity.

ISAIAH 34
Observation Worksheet

Chapter Theme _____

DRAW near, O nations, to hear; and listen, O peoples!

    Let the earth and all it contains hear, and the world and all that springs from it.

2   For the LORD's indignation is against all the nations,

    And *His* wrath against all their armies;

    He has utterly destroyed them,

    He has given them over to slaughter.

3   So their slain will be thrown out,

    And their corpses will give off their stench,

    And the mountains will be drenched with their blood.

4   And all the host of heaven will wear away,

    And the sky will be rolled up like a scroll;

    All their hosts will also wither away

    As a leaf withers from the vine,

    Or as *one* withers from the fig tree.

5   For My sword is satiated in heaven,

    Behold it shall descend for judgment upon Edom

    And upon the people whom I have devoted to destruction.

6   The sword of the LORD is filled with blood,

    It is sated with fat, with the blood of lambs and goats,

    With the fat of the kidneys of rams.

    For the LORD has a sacrifice in Bozrah

    And a great slaughter in the land of Edom.

7   Wild oxen will also fall with them

    And young bulls with strong ones;

    Thus their land will be soaked with blood,

    And their dust become greasy with fat.

8   For the LORD has a day of vengeance,

    A year of recompense for the cause of Zion.

9   Its streams will be turned into pitch,

And its loose earth into brimstone,

And its land will become burning pitch.

10 It will not be quenched night or day;

Its smoke will go up forever.

From generation to generation it will be desolate;

None will pass through it forever and ever.

11 But pelican and hedgehog will possess it,

And owl and raven will dwell in it;

And He will stretch over it the line of desolation

And the plumb line of emptiness.

12 Its nobles—there is no one there

Whom they may proclaim king—

And all its princes will be nothing.

13 Thorns will come up in its fortified towers,

Nettles and thistles in its fortified cities;

It will also be a haunt of jackals

And an abode of ostriches.

14 The desert creatures will meet with the wolves,

The hairy goat also will cry to its kind;

Yes, the night monster will settle there

And will find herself a resting place.

15 The tree snake will make its nest and lay *eggs* there,

And it will hatch and gather *them* under its protection.

Yes, the hawks will be gathered there,

Every one with its kind.

16 Seek from the book of the LORD, and read:

Not one of these will be missing;

None will lack its mate.

For His mouth has commanded,

And His Spirit has gathered them.

17 He has cast the lot for them,

And His hand has divided it to them by line.

They shall possess it forever;

From generation to generation they will dwell in it.

ISAIAH 35
Observation Worksheet

Chapter Theme _____

THE wilderness and the desert will be glad,

    And the Arabah will rejoice and blossom;

    Like the crocus

2   It will blossom profusely

    And rejoice with rejoicing and shout of joy.

    The glory of Lebanon will be given to it,

    The majesty of Carmel and Sharon.

    They will see the glory of the LORD,

    The majesty of our God.

3   Encourage the exhausted, and strengthen the feeble.

4   Say to those with anxious heart,

    "Take courage, fear not.

    Behold, your God will come *with* vengeance;

    The recompense of God will come,

    But He will save you."

5   Then the eyes of the blind will be opened

    And the ears of the deaf will be unstopped.

6   Then the lame will leap like a deer,

    And the tongue of the mute will shout for joy.

    For waters will break forth in the wilderness

    And streams in the Arabah.

7   The scorched land will become a pool

    And the thirsty ground springs of water;

    In the haunt of jackals, its resting place,

    Grass *becomes* reeds and rushes.

8   A highway will be there, a roadway,

    And it will be called the Highway of Holiness.

    The unclean will not travel on it,

    But it *will* be for him who walks *that* way,

    And fools will not wander *on it*.

9   No lion will be there,
         Nor will any vicious beast go up on it;
         These will not be found there.
         But the redeemed will walk *there,*

10   And the ransomed of the LORD will return
         And come with joyful shouting to Zion,
         With everlasting joy upon their heads.
         They will find gladness and joy,
         And sorrow and sighing will flee away.

ISAIAH 36
Observation Worksheet

Chapter Theme _____

NOW in the fourteenth year of King Hezekiah, Sennacherib king of Assyria came up against all the fortified cities of Judah and seized them.

2   And the king of Assyria sent Rabshakeh from Lachish to Jerusalem to King Hezekiah with a large army. And he stood by the conduit of the upper pool on the highway of the fuller's field.

3   Then Eliakim the son of Hilkiah, who was over the household, and Shebna the scribe, and Joah the son of Asaph, the recorder, came out to him.

4   Then Rabshakeh said to them, "Say now to Hezekiah, 'Thus says the great king, the king of Assyria, "What is this confidence that you have?

5   "I say, 'Your counsel and strength for the war are only empty words.' Now on whom do you rely, that you have rebelled against me?

6   "Behold, you rely on the staff of this crushed reed, *even* on Egypt, on which if a man leans, it will go into his hand and pierce it. So is Pharaoh king of Egypt to all who rely on him.

7   "But if you say to me, 'We trust in the LORD our God,' is it not He whose high places and whose altars Hezekiah has taken away and has said to Judah and to Jerusalem, 'You shall worship before this altar'?

8   "Now therefore, come make a bargain with my master the king of Assyria, and I will give you two thousand horses, if you are able on your part to set riders on them.

9   "How then can you repulse one official of the least of my master's servants and rely on Egypt for chariots and for horsemen?

10 "Have I now come up without the LORD's approval against this land to destroy it? The LORD said to me, 'Go up against this land and destroy it.' " ' "

11 Then Eliakim and Shebna and Joah said to Rabshakeh, "Speak now to your servants in Aramaic, for we understand *it;* and do not speak with us in Judean in the hearing of the people who are on the wall."

12 But Rabshakeh said, "Has my master sent me only to your master and to you to speak these words, *and* not to the men who sit on the wall, *doomed* to eat their own dung and drink their own urine with you?"

13   Then Rabshakeh stood and cried with a loud voice in Judean and said, "Hear the words of the great king, the king of Assyria.

14   "Thus says the king, 'Do not let Hezekiah deceive you, for he will not be able to deliver you;

15   nor let Hezekiah make you trust in the LORD, saying, "The LORD will surely deliver us, this city will not be given into the hand of the king of Assyria."

16   'Do not listen to Hezekiah,' for thus says the king of Assyria, 'Make your peace with me and come out to me, and eat each of his vine and each of his fig tree and drink each of the waters of his own cistern,

17   until I come and take you away to a land like your own land, a land of grain and new wine, a land of bread and vineyards.

18   '*Beware* that Hezekiah does not mislead you, saying, "The LORD will deliver us." Has any one of the gods of the nations delivered his land from the hand of the king of Assyria?

19   'Where are the gods of Hamath and Arpad? Where are the gods of Sepharvaim? And when have they delivered Samaria from my hand?

20   'Who among all the gods of these lands have delivered their land from my hand, that the LORD would deliver Jerusalem from my hand?' "

21   But they were silent and answered him not a word; for the king's commandment was, "Do not answer him."

22   Then Eliakim the son of Hilkiah, who was over the household, and Shebna the scribe and Joah the son of Asaph, the recorder, came to Hezekiah with their clothes torn and told him the words of Rabshakeh.

ISAIAH 37
Observation Worksheet

Chapter Theme _____

AND when King Hezekiah heard *it,* he tore his clothes, covered himself with sackcloth and entered the house of the LORD.

2 Then he sent Eliakim who was over the household with Shebna the scribe and the elders of the priests, covered with sackcloth, to Isaiah the prophet, the son of Amoz.

3 They said to him, "Thus says Hezekiah, 'This day is a day of distress, rebuke and rejection; for children have come to birth, and there is no strength to deliver.

4 'Perhaps the LORD your God will hear the words of Rabshakeh, whom his master the king of Assyria has sent to reproach the living God, and will rebuke the words which the LORD your God has heard. Therefore, offer a prayer for the remnant that is left.' "

5 So the servants of King Hezekiah came to Isaiah.

6 Isaiah said to them, "Thus you shall say to your master, 'Thus says the LORD, "Do not be afraid because of the words that you have heard, with which the servants of the king of Assyria have blasphemed Me.

7 "Behold, I will put a spirit in him so that he will hear a rumor and return to his own land. And I will make him fall by the sword in his own land." ' "

8 Then Rabshakeh returned and found the king of Assyria fighting against Libnah, for he had heard that the king had left Lachish.

9 When he heard *them* say concerning Tirhakah king of Cush, "He has come out to fight against you," and when he heard *it* he sent messengers to Hezekiah, saying,

10 "Thus you shall say to Hezekiah king of Judah, 'Do not let your God in whom you trust deceive you, saying, "Jerusalem will not be given into the hand of the king of Assyria."

11 'Behold, you have heard what the kings of Assyria have done to all the lands, destroying them completely. So will you be spared?

12 'Did the gods of those nations which my fathers have destroyed deliver them, *even* Gozan and Haran and Rezeph and the sons of Eden who *were* in Telassar?

13 'Where is the king of Hamath, the king of Arpad, the king of the city of Sepharvaim, *and of* Hena and Ivvah?' "

14 Then Hezekiah took the letter from the hand of the messengers and read it, and he went up to the house of the LORD and spread it out before the LORD.

15 Hezekiah prayed to the LORD saying,

16 "O Lord of hosts, the God of Israel, who is enthroned *above* the cherubim, You are the God, You alone, of all the kingdoms of the earth. You have made heaven and earth.

17 "Incline Your ear, O Lord, and hear; open Your eyes, O Lord, and see; and listen to all the words of Sennacherib, who sent *them* to reproach the living God.

18 "Truly, O Lord, the kings of Assyria have devastated all the countries and their lands,

19 and have cast their gods into the fire, for they were not gods but the work of men's hands, wood and stone. So they have destroyed them.

20 "Now, O Lord our God, deliver us from his hand that all the kingdoms of the earth may know that You alone, Lord, are God."

21 Then Isaiah the son of Amoz sent *word* to Hezekiah, saying, "Thus says the Lord, the God of Israel, 'Because you have prayed to Me about Sennacherib king of Assyria,

22 this is the word that the Lord has spoken against him:

"She has despised you and mocked you,

The virgin daughter of Zion;

She has shaken *her* head behind you,

The daughter of Jerusalem!

23 "Whom have you reproached and blasphemed?

And against whom have you raised *your* voice

And haughtily lifted up your eyes?

Against the Holy One of Israel!

24 "Through your servants you have reproached the Lord,

And you have said, 'With my many chariots I came up to the heights of the mountains,

To the remotest parts of Lebanon;

And I cut down its tall cedars *and* its choice cypresses.

And I will go to its highest peak, its thickest forest.

25 'I dug *wells* and drank waters,

And with the sole of my feet I dried up

All the rivers of Egypt.'

26 "Have you not heard?

Long ago I did it,

From ancient times I planned it.

Now I have brought it to pass,

That you should turn fortified cities into ruinous heaps.

27 "Therefore their inhabitants were short of strength,

They were dismayed and put to shame;

They were *as* the vegetation of the field and *as* the green herb,

As grass on the housetops is scorched before it is grown up.

28 "But I know your sitting down

And your going out and your coming in

And your raging against Me.

29 "Because of your raging against Me

And because your arrogance has come up to My ears,

Therefore I will put My hook in your nose

And My bridle in your lips,

And I will turn you back by the way which you came.

30 "Then this shall be the sign for you: you will eat this year what grows of itself, in the second year what springs from the same, and in the third year sow, reap, plant vineyards and eat their fruit.

31 "The surviving remnant of the house of Judah will again take root downward and bear fruit upward.

32 "For out of Jerusalem will go forth a remnant and out of Mount Zion survivors. The zeal of the LORD of hosts will perform this." '

33 "Therefore, thus says the LORD concerning the king of Assyria, 'He will not come to this city or shoot an arrow there; and he will not come before it with a shield, or throw up a siege ramp against it.

34 'By the way that he came, by the same he will return, and he will not come to this city,' declares the LORD.

35 'For I will defend this city to save it for My own sake and for My servant David's sake.' "

36 Then the angel of the LORD went out and struck 185,000 in the camp of the Assyrians; and when men arose early in the morning, behold, all of these were dead.

37 So Sennacherib king of Assyria departed and returned *home* and lived at Nineveh.

38 It came about as he was worshiping in the house of Nisroch his god, that Adrammelech and Sharezer his sons killed him with the sword; and they escaped into the land of Ararat. And Esarhaddon his son became king in his place.

Chapter Theme _____

IN those days Hezekiah became mortally ill. And Isaiah the prophet the son of Amoz came to him and said to him, "Thus says the LORD, 'Set your house in order, for you shall die and not live.' "

2   Then Hezekiah turned his face to the wall and prayed to the LORD,

3   and said, "Remember now, O LORD, I beseech You, how I have walked before You in truth and with a whole heart, and have done what is good in Your sight." And Hezekiah wept bitterly.

4   Then the word of the LORD came to Isaiah, saying,

5   "Go and say to Hezekiah, 'Thus says the LORD, the God of your father David, "I have heard your prayer, I have seen your tears; behold, I will add fifteen years to your life.

6   "I will deliver you and this city from the hand of the king of Assyria; and I will defend this city." '

7   "This shall be the sign to you from the LORD, that the LORD will do this thing that He has spoken:

8   "Behold, I will cause the shadow on the stairway, which has gone down with the sun on the stairway of Ahaz, to go back ten steps." So the sun's *shadow* went back ten steps on the stairway on which it had gone down.

9   A writing of Hezekiah king of Judah after his illness and recovery:

10   I said, "In the middle of my life
      I am to enter the gates of Sheol;
      I am to be deprived of the rest of my years."

11   I said, "I will not see the LORD,
      The LORD in the land of the living;
      I will look on man no more among the inhabitants of the world.

12   "Like a shepherd's tent my dwelling is pulled up and removed from me;
      As a weaver I rolled up my life.
      He cuts me off from the loom;
      From day until night You make an end of me.

13   "I composed *my soul* until morning.
      Like a lion—so He breaks all my bones,
      From day until night You make an end of me.

14   "Like a swallow, *like* a crane, so I twitter;

        I moan like a dove;

        My eyes look wistfully to the heights;

        O Lord, I am oppressed, be my security.

15   "What shall I say?

        For He has spoken to me, and He Himself has done it;

        I will wander about all my years because of the bitterness of my soul.

16   "O Lord, by *these* things *men* live,

        And in all these is the life of my spirit;

        O restore me to health and let me live!

17   "Lo, for *my own* welfare I had great bitterness;

        It is You who has kept my soul from the pit of nothingness,

        For You have cast all my sins behind Your back.

18   "For Sheol cannot thank You,

        Death cannot praise You;

        Those who go down to the pit cannot hope for Your faithfulness.

19   "It is the living who give thanks to You, as I do today;

        A father tells his sons about Your faithfulness.

20   "The LORD will surely save me;

        So we will play my songs on stringed instruments

        All *the* days of our life at the house of the LORD."

21   Now Isaiah had said, "Let them take a cake of figs and apply it to the boil, that he may recover."

22   Then Hezekiah had said, "What is the sign that I shall go up to the house of the LORD?"

ISAIAH 39
Observation Worksheet

Chapter Theme _____

AT that time Merodach-baladan son of Baladan, king of Babylon, sent letters and a present to Hezekiah, for he heard that he had been sick and had recovered.

2 Hezekiah was pleased, and showed them *all* his treasure house, the silver and the gold and the spices and the precious oil and his whole armory and all that was found in his treasuries. There was nothing in his house nor in all his dominion that Hezekiah did not show them.

3 Then Isaiah the prophet came to King Hezekiah and said to him, "What did these men say, and from where have they come to you?" And Hezekiah said, "They have come to me from a far country, from Babylon."

4 He said, "What have they seen in your house?" So Hezekiah answered, "They have seen all that is in my house; there is nothing among my treasuries that I have not shown them."

5 Then Isaiah said to Hezekiah, "Hear the word of the LORD of hosts,

6 'Behold, the days are coming when all that is in your house and all that your fathers have laid up in store to this day will be carried to Babylon; nothing will be left,' says the LORD.

7 'And *some* of your sons who will issue from you, whom you will beget, will be taken away, and they will become officials in the palace of the king of Babylon.' "

8 Then Hezekiah said to Isaiah, "The word of the LORD which you have spoken is good." For he thought, "For there will be peace and truth in my days."

ISAIAH 40
Observation Worksheet

Chapter Theme _____

"COMFORT, O comfort My people," says your God.

2   "Speak kindly to Jerusalem;

And call out to her, that her warfare has ended,

That her iniquity has been removed,

That she has received of the LORD's hand

Double for all her sins."

3   A voice is calling,

"Clear the way for the LORD in the wilderness;

Make smooth in the desert a highway for our God.

4   "Let every valley be lifted up,

And every mountain and hill be made low;

And let the rough ground become a plain,

And the rugged terrain a broad valley;

5   Then the glory of the LORD will be revealed,

And all flesh will see *it* together;

For the mouth of the LORD has spoken."

6   A voice says, "Call out."

Then he answered, "What shall I call out?"

All flesh is grass, and all its loveliness is like the flower of the field.

7   The grass withers, the flower fades,

When the breath of the LORD blows upon it;

Surely the people are grass.

8   The grass withers, the flower fades,

But the word of our God stands forever.

9   Get yourself up on a high mountain,

O Zion, bearer of good news,

Lift up your voice mightily,

O Jerusalem, bearer of good news;

Lift *it* up, do not fear.

Say to the cities of Judah,

"Here is your God!"

10   Behold, the Lord God will come with might,

With His arm ruling for Him.

Behold, His reward is with Him

And His recompense before Him.

11   Like a shepherd He will tend His flock,

In His arm He will gather the lambs

And carry *them* in His bosom;

He will gently lead the nursing *ewes*.

12   Who has measured the waters in the hollow of His hand,

And marked off the heavens by the span,

And calculated the dust of the earth by the measure,

And weighed the mountains in a balance

And the hills in a pair of scales?

13   Who has directed the Spirit of the Lord,

Or as His counselor has informed Him?

14   With whom did He consult and *who* gave Him understanding?

And *who* taught Him in the path of justice and taught Him knowledge

And informed Him of the way of understanding?

15   Behold, the nations are like a drop from a bucket,

And are regarded as a speck of dust on the scales;

Behold, He lifts up the islands like fine dust.

16   Even Lebanon is not enough to burn,

Nor its beasts enough for a burnt offering.

17   All the nations are as nothing before Him,

They are regarded by Him as less than nothing and meaningless.

18   To whom then will you liken God?

Or what likeness will you compare with Him?

19   *As for* the idol, a craftsman casts it,

A goldsmith plates it with gold,

And a silversmith *fashions* chains of silver.

20   He who is too impoverished for *such* an offering

Selects a tree that does not rot;

He seeks out for himself a skillful craftsman

To prepare an idol that will not totter.

21   Do you not know? Have you not heard?

Has it not been declared to you from the beginning?

Have you not understood from the foundations of the earth?

22   It is He who sits above the circle of the earth,

And its inhabitants are like grasshoppers,

Who stretches out the heavens like a curtain

And spreads them out like a tent to dwell in.

23   He *it is* who reduces rulers to nothing,

Who makes the judges of the earth meaningless.

24   Scarcely have they been planted,

Scarcely have they been sown,

Scarcely has their stock taken root in the earth,

But He merely blows on them, and they wither,

And the storm carries them away like stubble.

25   "To whom then will you liken Me

That I would be *his* equal?" says the Holy One.

26   Lift up your eyes on high

And see who has created these *stars,*

The One who leads forth their host by number,

He calls them all by name;

Because of the greatness of His might and the strength of *His* power,

Not one *of them* is missing.

27   Why do you say, O Jacob, and assert, O Israel,

"My way is hidden from the Lord,

And the justice due me escapes the notice of my God"?

28   Do you not know? Have you not heard?

The Everlasting God, the Lord, the Creator of the ends of the earth

Does not become weary or tired.

His understanding is inscrutable.

29   He gives strength to the weary,

And to *him who* lacks might He increases power.

30   Though youths grow weary and tired,

And vigorous young men stumble badly,

31 Yet those who wait for the LORD
  Will gain new strength;
  They will mount up *with* wings like eagles,
  They will run and not get tired,
  They will walk and not become weary

My Take-away Truths From This Study

_____

_____

_____

_____

_____

_____

_____

_____

_____

_____

_____

_____

_____

_____

_____

_____

_____

_____

_____

_____

_____

_____

_____

_____

My Take-away Truths From This Study

_____
_____
_____
_____
_____
_____
_____
_____
_____
_____
_____
_____
_____
_____
_____
_____
_____
_____
_____
_____
_____
_____
_____
_____
_____
_____
_____
_____

DISCOVER TRUTH FOR YOURSELF

Our passion is for you to discover Truth for yourself through Inductive Bible Study—a unique Bible study method you'll discover in the following pages and use throughout this study, as we engage this important topic together verse by verse.

You can't do a better thing than sit at Jesus' feet, listening to His every word. God's Word, the Bible, has answers for every situation you'll face in life. Listen to what God is saying to you, face-to-face, with truth to transform your life!

INDUCTIVE BIBLE STUDY METHOD

To study and understand God's Word, we use the Inductive Bible Study Method at Precept Ministries International. The Bible is our main source of truth. Before looking for insights from people and commentaries *about* the Bible, we get into the Word of God, beginning with observing the text.

❶ Observation

This is a very interactive process, well worth the time because the truths you discover for yourself will be accurate and profound. It begins by asking the five W and H questions.

Who is speaking? Who is this about? Who are the main characters? And to whom is the speaker speaking?

What subjects and/or events are covered in the chapter? What do you learn about the people, the events, and the teachings from the text? What instructions are given?

When did or will the events recorded occur?

Where did or will this happen? Where was it said?

Why is something said? Why will an event occur? Why this time, person, and/or place?

How will it happen? How will it be done? How is it illustrated?

Careful observation leads to interpretation—discovering what the text means.

❷ Interpretation

The more you observe, the greater you'll understand God's Word. Since Scripture is the best interpreter of Scripture, you and I will be looking at contexts and cross-references to enhance our understanding of the meaning of God's message.

Where should observation and interpretation lead? Application.

❸ Application

After we've observed the text and discovered what it means, we need to think and live accordingly. The result is a transformed life—the more you and I are in the Word of God and adjusting our thinking and behavior to its precepts for life, the more we are changed into the likeness of Jesus Christ! He is the living Word of God who became flesh, the Savior of the world, our coming King of kings!

SO WHERE DO YOU BEGIN?

The Bible is *God's* book, His Word, so when you study it you need to seek the Author's help. Begin with prayer, asking God to lead you into all truth, then open the Study Companion. (We suggest you work one program ahead of the broadcast to get the most out of the study.) Look at the general layout of each day's program and you will find the following:

- Introduction—usually with a challenging question
- Questions that contain pointers on using the Inductive Bible Study Method
- **Where's That Verse?** section containing the Primary Study Passage and several cross-references related to the topic
- Concluding Prayer

WHAT'S NEXT?

- In some programs, I'll point out key words to mark. You'll find many of them on the back cover of this Study Companion with *suggested* colors and symbols to spot them quickly in the text. Color coding key words helps you identify and recall. We have included a cutout bookmark so you can remember to mark each key word the same way throughout the text.

  You can mark these key words before or after the program, whichever is easier. You can also get the CD or DVD of the program and mark the key words later while studying.

Feel free to mark them your own way—there's nothing sacred about the particular symbols and colors I use!

- The cross-references I mention in these programs are under **Where's That Verse?** After you read them, you can jot them in the margins of the **Observation Worksheets** or write them in the wide margins of your Bible. I suggest you first pencil them in, then write them in ink later.

- For book studies, you'll find an **At A Glance** chart in the back. After we complete a chapter, record a summary theme there and in the space provided in your **Observation Worksheets**. Themes help you remember main ideas of chapters **At A Glance** after you finish the study. You'll also find these charts after each book in the *New Inductive Study Bible*.

MISSED A PROGRAM?

- Go to our website at **www.PreceptsForLife.com**. TV viewers can call 1.800.763.1990 and radio listeners 1.888.734.7707 to learn how to find programs online.

GETTING THE MOST FROM THIS STUDY

- Try to stay one program ahead of me so you'll learn directly from the Word of God and our time together will be like a "discussion group," as we reason together through the Scriptures. You'll get much more out of our time together if you've done this preparation.

- Try to memorize a key verse for every program covered. God will bring these to your remembrance when you need them!

- Pray about what you learn each day. Ask God to remind you of these truths and give you another person to share them with. These two exercises will do amazing things in your life.

- Get the CD or DVD set of this series and listen when you get ready for work in the morning, do chores around the house, or have family devotions. Or listen with an open Bible and discuss the teaching and its application to your life. Get together with a friend, view or listen to a message, and discuss it or use it for family devotions. You can also view or listen programs online. Visit **www.PreceptsForLife.com.**

- Request Precept's mailings to stay abreast of what God is doing around the world and to pray for the needs we share with you. You can be a significant part of this unique global ministry God is using to establish people in His Word. Here are some items you can request:

- ✦ The *Plumbline*—Precept Ministry's monthly e-newsletter that keeps you up to date on Bible study topics, products and events that help you in your walk with Christ.

- ✦ A prayer list so you can partner with us in prayer for our ministries in nearly 150 countries and 70 languages.

- ✦ "Inside information" each month when you join our "E-Team" of regular prayer and financial supporters. Visit **www.PreceptsForLife.com** for more information on how you can support our programs. (You can check out the current monthly letter right now on our website.)

- ✦ Advance notice of conferences at our headquarters in Chattanooga and throughout the United States and Canada.

- ✦ Information about our study tours in Israel, Jordan, Greece, Turkey, and Italy, where we teach various books of the Bible right where the action occurred!

- • We use one of the most accurate translations of the Bible, the New American Standard (Updated). If the topic is a book study, our **Observation Worksheets** will contain the complete text. Since you'll be instructed to mark words and phrases and make notes in the text, you'll want to have colored pencils or pens available. As you grow in inductive study skills, you may want to use your Bible instead. We believe the best Bible to use is the *New Inductive Study Bible.* See our back pages to find out more about this ultimate study Bible. Now get started!

- • Finally, stay in touch with me personally. I'd so love to hear from you by email or letter so I can be sensitive to where you are and what you're experiencing—problems you're wrestling with, questions you have, etc. This will help me teach more effectively and personally. Just email us at info@precept.org. (Don't worry, Beloved, I won't mention you by name; but as you listen, you'll know I've heard you!)

I'm committed to you . . . because of Him. The purpose of the "Precepts For Life" TV & Radio programs is to help you realize your full potential in God, so you can become the exemplary believer God intends you to be…studying the Bible inductively, viewing the world biblically, making disciples intentionally, and serving the Church faithfully in the power of the Holy Spirit."

That's my vision for us as believers! Won't you help us spread it to others?

Looking for people…looking for truth!

How Do I Start Studying The Bible?

Do you wonder,
"God, how can I obey You and study your Word? Where do I begin? How can I discover truth
for myself?

DISCOVER TRUTH FOR YOURSELF

There are some study tools we would recommend for you to begin with, as each will teach you the inductive method of study. By inductive we mean that you can go straight to the Word of God and discover truth for yourself, so you can say … "for You, Yourself have taught me" (Psalm 119:102).

Let's Get Started! For a jump start on inductive study, we recommend the following:

- *Lord, Teach Me To Study The Bible in 28 Days.* In this hands-on introduction to the basics of inductive study, you'll see why you need to study God's Word and how to dig into the truths of a book of the Bible. The instructions will walk you through the books of Jonah and Jude, and you'll be awed at what you see on your own! Discussion questions are included.

- *God, Are You There? Do You Care? Do You Know About Me?* This 13-week, self-contained inductive study on the Gospel of John is powerful and life-changing. Study the book of John, as you learn and put into practice inductive study skills. The Gospel of John was written that you might believe that Jesus is the Son of God and that believing, might have life in His name. You will know you are loved! Discussion questions are included.

- *How to Study Old Testament History and Prophecy Workshop.* Discover truths about who God is and how He works as you learn to study inductively, step by step, and be challenged to apply these truths to your life. This workshop will give you the tools to study and understand Old Testament history and prophecy. Go to www.precept.org or call 800-763-8280 to find out about workshops in your area, or online training.

- *How to Study a New Testament Letter Workshop.* Grow in the knowledge of the Lord Jesus Christ and His plan for your life. This inductive study workshop will equip you to study the New Testament letters and apply their truths to your life. Go to www.precept. org or call 800-763-8280 to find out about workshops in your area, or online training.

Now that you've begun . . . continue studying inductively using one of these:

- *40 Minute Bible Studies.* These 6-week topical studies are a good for personal study and a great way to start discipling others one-on-one or in a group setting—teaching them who God is, introducing them to Jesus Christ, and helping them learn God's precepts for life. These studies enable you to discover what God says about different issues of life. No homework is necessary for the students prior to group time.

- *The New Inductive Study Series,* now complete covering every book of the Bible, was created to help you discover truth for yourself and go deeper into God's precepts, promises and purposes. This powerful series is ideal for personal study, small groups, Sunday school classes, family devotions, and discipling others. Containing 13-week long studies, the New

Inductive Study Series also provides easy planning for church curriculum! You can now survey the entire Bible

- *Lord Series.* These life-changing devotional studies cover in greater depth major issues of our relationship with God and with others, teaching us how to practically live out our faith. Ideal for small groups, these contain discussion guides and teaching DVDs are available for some.

- *Discover 4 Yourself* is a dynamic series of inductive studies for children. Children who can read learn how to discover truth for themselves through the life-impacting skills of observation, interpretation, and application. You'll be amazed at the change that comes when children know for themselves what the Word of God says! Teach them now so they can stand firm in a first-hand knowledge of truth as they hit their teen years. This award-winning series is popular in Christian schools and among homeschoolers. Teacher's guides are available online.

- *The New Inductive Study Bible (NISB)* is a unique and exciting! Most study Bibles give you someone else's interpretation of the text. The NISB doesn't tell you what to believe, rather it helps you discover truth for yourself by showing you how to study inductively and providing instructions, study helps, and application questions for each book of the Bible, as well as wide margins for your notes. It's filled with many wonderful features that will guide you toward the joy of discovering the truths of God's Word for yourself. This Bible is your legacy.

GO DEEPER WITH OTHERS... IN SMALL GROUP BIBLE STUDIES

Join others in the study of God's Word, sharing insights from the Scripture and discussing application to your life. Each of the studies described above are appropriate for groups as well as for individual study.

Discussion questions are included, so that you can dialogue about what you're learning with a group. These studies will teach you what it means to live by God's Word—and how it is applied to life. Learn about and discuss with others the truth that sets you free! To find out about inductive Bible study groups in your area, go to www.precept.org or call 800-763-8280.

DISCIPLE

How can you help others study God's Word inductively? Use the studies described above to share with others—one-on-one or in a small group. Lead others in discovering truth for themselves and experience the joy of seeing God change lives!

If you want training in how to lead these and other Precept Upon Precept studies go to www.precept.org or call us at 800-763-8280.

**Precept Ministries International | P.O. Box 182218 | Chattanooga, TN 37422
800.763.8280 | www.precept.org**

CPSIA information can be obtained
at www.ICGtesting.com
Printed in the USA
LVOW04s1944061117
555230LV00026B/456/P

9 781934 884409